For Here or To Go
Life in the Service Industry

Edited by Leah Ryan

For more information please address:
Garrett County Press, LLC.
828 Royal St. #248
New Orleans, LA 70116
www.gcpress.com

GCPress books are printed on acid free paper.

LIBRARY OF CONGRESS CATALOGING-IN-PUBLICATION DATA

Ryan, Leah
    For here or to go : life in the service industry / edited by Leah Ryan.
        1st ed.
        p. cm.
    ISBN 1-891053-44-2 (alk. paper)
    1. Service industries workers. I. Ryan, Leah, 1964-
    HD8039.S45F67 2004
    331.7'0092'2--dc22   2004002902

Garrett County Press first edition 2004

Text design by Meredith Martin,
iCONiKLaSTique Design Klinik, LLC
www.iDKdesign.com

Cover design by
Karen Ocker

Thanks...

to G.K. Darby of Garrett Country Press
for believing in this project and being patient

to Jeff Kelly of *Temp Slave* for inspiring me to undertake it in the first place

to Moira Gentry for her editorial genius

to my friends and family for their unwavering support, money or no money,
work or no work, smoking or non smoking... for helping me believe that all
the stuff I do is worth doing when I feel like giving up

and to every fellow worker who ever took the time
to teach me something.

Forward

I have wanted to do a book like this one for many years. Not so much to gripe, complain, or expose the evil establishment -- if those things happen as a by-product, so be it. But my motive was (and still is) to tell stories, and to create a place for stories to be told.

How many times have I been at work, or out in the world watching people work, and found myself thinking, 'Oh my god. I just wish someone could see this. Why is nobody watching this?'

I don't think that this book romanticizes work in the service industry. But among the ugly stories of low pay and sweaty, difficult work, there is another, more positive common thread: the ability that people have, regardless of their professions, to find something good in their work. It usually doesn't last, but that's often not the worker's fault. We've all seen the disgruntled worker stereotype: The pissed off clockwatcher leaning on his broom. The fed-up cook spitting in the food (a popular urban legend that I've never actually seen happen). The harried waitress throwing a quart of gravy on an innocent family of four. And now we have the postal worker jokes -- "Don't piss her off, or she'll go postal," and so on.

Of course sometimes it's this simple: Your job sucks, there's no joy in it whatsoever, the pay sucks, the boss sucks, it's pointless and horrible. But what's truly remarkable about many of the people I have known, and the people I've learned about since starting this project, is that they really care about their jobs. If you ask white-collar workers what they hate about their jobs, they'll often tell you about the thing that's preventing them from doing the best work they can do. Many service industry workers complain about the same things. No matter how crappy the job is, people tend to try to look for the higher good in what they do. And the perks are few and far between.

The stories in this volume span decades. The minimum wage was a little under three dollars an hour when I started working, in the late 1970s. Now, it's still only five dollars and fifteen cents an hour. The last time it went up was 1997. It barely budged during the Reagan/Daddy Bush years. Imagine working for a company, any company, for *thirty years*, while the cost of living skyrockets and your hourly wage, in those *thirty years,* increases by about three dollars per hour?

I have a feeling that if you took an informal poll of middle-class white-collar folks, a lot of them wouldn't be able to tell you what the minimum wage is, unless they have to deal with hiring and firing themselves. Even then, in the corporate world, a lot of that hiring and firing is handled by temp agencies. I have had numerous conversations with people who seem to think that the minimum wage is 10 or 12 dollars an hour. Where do they get this from? Why are they so misinformed?

We can blame some of it on media spin. Every day you read something about this mysterious beast called "the economy" and its constant companion, "the unemployment rate." Now and then we hear about a thing called "the poverty line." What does all this mean? I'm no economist, so I can't tell you. But I can tell you that to many working people, it doesn't mean a hell of a lot. Anyone living at the so-called "poverty line" is basically eating dirt. Many, many people hover above it, working like dogs, invisible and uncounted, and are what we non-economists like to call "fucking broke." The 1980s are often characterized as a time when everyone was making tons of money. I characterize it as a time when my rent doubled and I still made four or five bucks an hour. So I guess it depends on whom you ask. The cost of living increased for everyone, but not everyone reaped the benefits of that "economy."

But enough about the pay. What about the work, and the conditions of the work? How many people are aware that many restaurants don't allow their employees to eat at their places of employment? How many people realize that the waiter or waitress serving their dinner makes a flat hourly wage of two dollars and change, and relies on tips to bring that up to something approaching a living wage? What about the arbitrary and often backbreaking (and labor law--breaking) rules imposed by many restaurant owners (double shifts, no breaks)? What might have been going on in the mind of the last pizza delivery guy, messenger, or stripper you came in contact with?

About seven years ago, I moved to New York City, after spending my entire life in small towns whose economies revolved around academia and service. I'd spent my life, since the age of 16, in restaurant kitchens. Most of my friends worked in restaurants, in retail, and as housepainters. Everyone had sore backs and dirty fingernails.

Since coming to New York, I have not worked in the service industry at all. There are a few reasons for this. The primary reason is that New York's service economy revolves around immigrants. When I first arrived, I was advised to seek employment as a temp.

I did not do well as a temp. My typing skills are unorthodox, and I do not know how to dress corporate, casual or otherwise. I was disgusted (though not terribly surprised) to find that there was a very specific racial breakdown in most of the offices I worked in. The bosses were white men. The tech guys were Asian. Black men ran the mailroom. Apparently, they liked to have a white girl on the phone, and sometimes that white girl was me. But I knew I was in trouble when I was instructed by a higher-up white girl (presumably the assistant to the assistant to the white boss guy) on how to deal with the numerous messengers (all men, mostly non-white) who delivered Very Important Items to the office.

"You have to watch them every minute," I was told. "Don't let them use the bathroom."

There also seemed to be no arrangements made to tip the messengers. I was supposed to sign for the Very Important Item and bid the messenger farewell, Watching Him Every Minute. Surely I was not expected to tip the messenger out of my own pocket? I generally made about nine dollars an hour at these jobs, minus a half hour for lunch, which you simply cannot live on in New York unless you live in the far reaches of Queens in a one-bedroom apartment with 10 of your close friends and family members. I worried about this tipping issue a great deal. I prayed that the company had some kind of arrangement whereby it sent a check for the messengers at the end of the week or something. In retrospect, I doubt it. The messengers just didn't get tipped. If you have never seen a New York City bike messenger in action, I recommend it. Don't waste your time watching *Survivor* or *Fear Factor.*

So here I am, with clean fingernails, sitting on my ass, with a lunch break (30 minutes, unpaid, but still...) and a book to read, and I'm being told to treat the messengers, who are doing what I have thought of all my life as Real Work, as a lower life form. They were the only thing in the office lower than me, the temp receptionist (with the possible exception of a mailroom guy.)

> ### I started to see the relationship between server and served in our culture.

It was then that I really started to see the relationship between server and served in our culture. I was between worlds -- not really server anymore, but not quite served either. I had traded in my bad back and my callused hands for a kind of status that I didn't want, in an environment that made me outraged, furious, and depressed in turns.

And now, since getting my MFA, I teach. I've traded in one kind of low-rent existence for another. But really, there's no comparison. I pretty much go to the bathroom when I want, and nobody (with the exception of an occasional student) yells at me like I'm the stupidest piece of crap that ever drew breath. I work in conditions that a lot of people would find unacceptable: long commute, low pay, no job security, the works. Sure, I complain. But I keep it in perspective.

I have a new set of problems now. I go on a date with a guy (white collar to the core) who insists on paying but only wants to leave a 10 percent tip. My neighborhood gets more trendy and affluent by the minute, and increasingly, I watch the people around me treat service workers like crap. Simple pleasantries like "Please" and "Thank you" are abandoned, and commands are barked: "No starch in the shirt. Not too much milk in the coffee." What the hell is going on here?

Recently I was teaching a writing class to adults who live in a very affluent resort area. One of the students was writing something about Ireland (though not Irish herself) and we got on the subject of "The Irish." The students informed me that lots of young Irish had been coming from Ireland in recent years to work the high season in the area, cleaning hotel rooms and landscaping and waitressing and so on. Then one of the women said that she'd rented out her guest house to some young Irish workers last year. "Don't rent to them," she advised me. "They're dirty."

Apparently my last name (Ryan!) went right by her. But beyond that, I'm sure she'd never guess that a few years ago I made my living on my feet in a 110 degree kitchen cranking out Reuben sandwiches for college students or making pounds and pounds of whole wheat bread for hoards of manicured and acupunctured lefty lawyers and PhDs. I think Dirty Irish is a pretty fit description. I drank my share, too, don't ya know.

This woman clearly thought of herself as a pretty decent person, and this is the clincher: if you can convince yourself that certain people are not quite human, you can easily exploit and insult them while still thinking of yourself as a pretty decent person. The wider the gap between rich and poor, the easier this becomes. It's way too easy now, and we're all paying a price.

This book is in no way meant to be a comprehensive economic or demographic study. I chose the stories for their gritty details and for their humanity: starving busboys, exhausted exotic dancers, humiliated waitresses with aching feet.

If you've been there, or you're there now, I hope you can feel some kinship with the writers in this book, and I hope you can find some identification (and maybe a couple of laughs) within its pages. I also hope you feel encouraged to write your own story, if you are so inclined.

If you haven't been there, I hope you will feel inspired to dig a little deeper for that tip, to remember to say "please" and "thank you," to remember that the people who serve you are made up of the same stuff as you. Don't be seduced by the idea that you are somehow genetically superior. Don't kid yourself that you're "skilled" and they're not (I challenge anyone in corporate America to wait tables or wash dishes for a day and see how "skilled" you are). Don't forget that you might have the power to make or break someone's day. When they're decompressing at the end of their shift (or shifts) be a good story for them to tell their coworkers or spouse or friends, not a bad one.

Leah Ryan, 2004

© 2003 Karen Ocker

A Quiet Place
Valina Persaud with Leah Ryan

Q: How old were you when you came here from Guyana?

A: I was 17.

Q: Did you speak English?

A: Only broken English.

Q: How did you learn?

A: I just learned as I went.

Q: It must have been overwhelming.

A: It was just too many things to deal with. At home there was no electricity, no running water. When it flooded you took a boat to school and you had to hold your uniform up so it wouldn't get wet. The only sounds you would hear at night were coconuts and mangoes falling out of the trees. Unless someone was breaking into your house.

Q: Did you start working right away when you came to the United States?

A: I had to, because my mother wasn't working. First I sold clothes at a mall in Jamaica (Queens). They were cheap clothes, bright colors. You know what I'm talking about. I was in a GED program then so I worked part-time. Then my grandmother got me another part-time job baby-sitting, but the child's father cornered me in the kitchen one day and said he wanted to "give me a hug." He tried to kiss me. That was the end of that. Then I had a job for the summer working with mentally disabled adults. This was my first time away from my family. The job was exhausting. You had to do everything for the people. It was a 24-hour job. But I loved it because you had to leave all your prejudices and ideas behind and just function in their world. That was just for the summer. Then later I worked at <u>Hudson News</u> at JFK [airport].

Q: How did you get that job?

A: My sister went to this job fair and signed us up for airport jobs. We thought we would be interviewing for security jobs or flight attendants or something. I had to write all these fake letters of recommendation. Then I got an interview with this tall white guy. He told me I'd be working for Hudson News.

Q: I always wondered about that. It seems like the people working at Hudson News are always Indian.

A: Yes. The place was filthy, everyone was Indian, and they said I'd be working in the "bookstore" because I was educated.

Q: What kind of bookstore was it?

A: They just had novels, and not good ones. A few classics like <u>Anna Karenina</u>. But anyway, I never worked there. I worked at a newsstand. My first day, I was alone, and I was really hungry so I ate a candy. They never said anything, but I'm sure they had me on camera. At first they told me I could read at work and then they took it back. The uniform was a tie and a cap. I wore the tie, but when they handed me the cap I said, "No way I'm wearing that." Because it looks stupid and who's going to talk to you when you look like that? My supervisor was also Guyanese, this little Indian lady. She said I talked too much to the customers. Then she started to gossip about me, saying I was a whore.

Q: You were a whore for talking?

A: Well, yes. I talked to men, and I talked to American women who looked, you know, loose. I was considered flirtatious.

Q: That's tricky. You have to talk to people at that job, and if you do, you're a whore.

A: I liked talking to people. At the airport, you have this moment with people and then you usually never see them again. Then I got into a big fight with the supervisor because she was taking forever to refund a customer's money and the customer had a plane to catch. She had paid for a *Times* and we were out. She [the customer] had just graduated from college and her family was sending her on a trip. She started to say, "It's only seventy-five cents, forget it," but that made me really angry. That's not right.

Q: It sounds like the supervisor wasn't very good at the job.

A: She wasn't. But she was passive and kissed ass, and the white bosses like that.

Q: What would be your dream job?

A: Teaching, but not in this school system we have now. I would also like to run a house where women could come just to rest their heads. All kinds of women. You wouldn't have to give any information about yourself. It would be just a quiet place, a place to rest.

Photograph by Elizabeth O'Connor

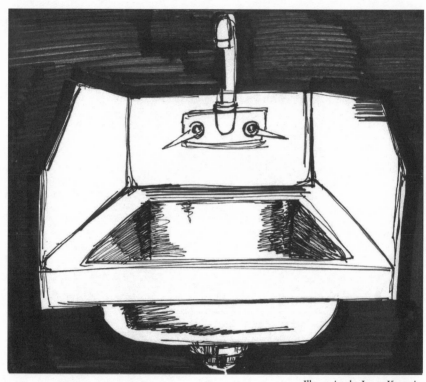

Illustration by Laura Kogonis

MOTEL ON HIGHWAY 29
Angelene J. Hall

The restaurant looked like a white boxcar. Situated between two horizontal rows of small dingy white red-shuttered motel rooms with paint curling and cracking like a late autumn leaf, the restaurant claimed to be the best eating-place in the county. Jones Motel was the only lodging within a 20-mile radius and people were always talking about how neat and clean the colored women kept the rooms. Of course, they couldn't eat or sleep there since the motel was white only, but it was one of the few places in the county where they could get a job "working for the public," which is what they called any job outside sharecropping. Lena heard from her mother and her aunt, who were the cleaning women, that Mr. Jones, the owner, had fired his last cook for what he termed, "a minor indiscretion," and her mother thought that since she was a good cook, she might as well apply for the job.

When Lena went to the restaurant to fill out the application, the motel owner's wife interviewed her. "My husband, he's a busy man and he wants me to do this," the woman said. Marge Jones, a tall stout ruddy-faced woman with yellowish-gray hair and liquor on her breath, said she was in charge of the restaurant and she was the one to do the hiring. Her husband had too much to handle with trying to keep his lodging business going and making sure the rooms were always "up to code." Lena knew what "up to code" meant because she had heard her mother and aunt talking about how G. Carter (which is what they called him behind his back) spent most of his time following them, checking to see if they stole anything. "Up to code" was just another way of saying his cleaning women weren't stealing any of the motel's old raggedy sheets and towels. The women liked calling him G. Carter because when his daddy was living, the Jones family lived in G. Carter trailer park. Lena's mother and aunt teased that G. Carter and Marge probably still lived there when they weren't shacked up in one of those old shitty motel rooms.

"How come you ain't up north somewhere doing something to make some real money? This 1959, girl. Tell me a women can git good jobs up north, 'specially colored girls." Marge Jones eyed Lena curiously. "Where you been?"

"Well, me and my husband live up the road there on Saddler's Place." Lena wondered what the woman was talking about. What did she mean, where had she had been?

"You married?"

"Yes, Ma'am."

"He working?"

"Yes, Ma'am.

"Doing what?" With a devilish smile, Marge Jones tilted her head and raised her brow.

"We farm. Or at least we did before that storm came through. Now he trying to find work just like me."

"Yeah," the woman said, changing her expression and pulling out a cigarette. "That goddam storm took the roof off one of them there motel rooms out yonder." Waving a flaming cigarette lighter, its blaze alternately shimmering red and yellow, she pointed to the outside and then lit her cigarette. "Well, anyway, you know we been mighty lucky to have Elnora and Aggie cleaning these rooms. They good, hard-working colored women, and I wouldn't take nothing for neither one of them. Can't nobody clean them rooms like them two. And every colored woman I know can cook. Why just the other day, I said to Aggie that I didn't know why she didn't take the cooking job. Can't nobody cook like colored women." She pulled on her cigarette and blew circles of smoke in the air. "They both praise you. Aggie say you the best for the cook. She say she know you can cook, cause she taught you." She laughed and looked at Lena. "Got any children?"

"Yes Ma'am. Three." Hugging her purse to her chest, Lena wasn't sure she wanted to work for a woman who believed that all colored women were good for was cooking and cleaning, and a man who thought they were all thieves. But what were her choices? When she tried to get a job at the tobacco factory, they told her to come back two days later when they would be hiring coloreds. When she returned, the line snaked so far ahead of her, with first white and then colored, she could hardly see the building. Before the line was half gone with still a few whites at the front, a white man came out raising a sign, NO MORE JOBS. The only other thing she had heard about was cleaning the restrooms in the courthouse, and she didn't think she could bear that kind of job because she knew how nasty some white folks could be. So, here she was sitting in the kitchen of the Jones Motel, waiting to see if she would get a job.

Lena had wanted to be a teacher. Ever since she was a child in the first grade, she had imagined herself in front of a class telling the children all about the fun of learning, just as her teacher had told her. But when she was in the 10th grade, her father had a heart attack and died after three days in the hospital. She dropped out of school to help her mother finish out the year's crops because Mr. Warner, the landowner, said there was no other way. So she postponed her dream. The next thing she knew she was married with three children and asking herself, "How in the world did I get to this place?"

"You sure you want this job? A woman with your looks could do a whole lot of things," Marge Jones said, half-smiling. "You know what I mean?" She reached over and shook Lena's shoulder. "Wish I looked good as you."

Now she thinks I'm a streetwalker, Lena thought, propping her elbow on the small table and gazing at the woman's arm. It was pale pink, fleshy, with a loose top layer of skin that draped over her arm. She wondered if the top layer were pulled back, would there be another less meaty layer. What was there underneath that thin flab that shook every time the woman moved?

"You listening to me?" The woman tapped Lena's shoulder again.

Lena jumped slightly and smiled. "Oh, yes Ma'am." She hoped the woman had not asked her anything important.

"You 'bout how old? I bet you ain't no more than 20."

"Twenty-four," Lena said.

Marge Jones leaned back in her chair and pulled on the cigarette. "Twenty-four, huh?" She folded her arms across her chest and leaned back, smiling to herself. "Ah! To be 20-something. What I'd give to be 20-something again." Then, straightening up as if she were coming out of a dream she didn't want to talk about, she looked at Lena out of the corner of her eyes. "I don't want to hire you today and you quit next week, just soon as something better come along."

Something better, Lena thought. She couldn't believe this woman expected loyalty and she hadn't even begun working yet. She wouldn't even be here if she thought there were something better for her now.

"What about crop time? You going to quit on us then?"

"Oh no, Ma'am," she said. "We not planning to farm after this year."

"Well, we pay $15 a week, and that's pretty goddam good, if you ask me. Besides your tips, and you'll git good tips, you can eat two meals a day in the kitchen, but I don't want to catch you taking nothing home. Me and Mr. Jones don't allow that. And there's a toilet out back behind the kitchen for the help." She pointed toward the back of the restaurant.

"Yes, Ma'am," Lena said with no particular expression. She had expected at least $20, but what could she do? $15 would not go very far, but at least it was more than she could see at one time working in Saddler's fields.

"Git paid every Thursday. Got Wednesdays off. Closed on Sundays. Got any questions, just ask me. Don't worry Mr. Jones 'bout it. Mind your business, and stay out of the motel rooms." The woman scooted her chair from the table with a loud scrape and stood up. "That's what got the last one fired. Out there fucking in one of the motel rooms and I caught her in the act." She shook her head, laughing. "You start tomorrow."

Lena was still calm as she stood up. She had shown no curiosity with the woman's comment about the last cook, but she was dying to know if she was colored or white. Didn't sound like no colored woman, at least she didn't think so. The last thing she needed was to come in behind that kind of thing, especially when white folks were always ready to think the worst anyway. She'd ask her aunt, Elnora. If anybody knew, she did.

Lena's orientation into the restaurant business lasted about two days, and it was less than a week before she realized it was criminal to pay her $15 a week for the amount of work she did. Arriving every morning between six and six-thirty, she had to wash any dishes the Jones' might have left in the sink from the night before. Rarely was there a morning when Mrs. Jones had not left a lipstick-stained cup or glass on the worktable in the kitchen, and an ashtray spilling over with twisted cigarette butts and ashes on one of the oilcloth-covered tables. By the time she cleaned up their mess and started the business for the morning, the crew from the rock quarry farther south on 29 was coming through the screen door.

The rock quarry crew was her daily dread. Covered with red dust when the weather was dry and mud up to their knees when it rained, they stomped into the restaurant, barking out their orders like drunken soldiers. All the while she prepared their typical morning meal of eggs, fatback, bread and coffee, G. Carter followed on her heels reminding her, "one egg to a order, a pan of bread to a table." Through the crew's joking with each other and calling for two and three orders, they ran Lena back and forth from the kitchen to the dining area until the soles of her feet burned, and never did they leave more than a 25 or 30 cent tip.

The crew, though, was just the beginning of the day. There were always those few people from the county who came in every other day or so just to have somewhere to go and because they enjoyed the cooking. They gobbled their food in a few minutes, but they lingered over the coffee for hours, constantly requesting a warm-up and then finally getting up and leaving nothing but the empty cups and dirty plates.

The restaurant was grueling work. Not only did Lena do all the cooking, but also she waited the tables, washed the dishes, did most of the food ordering, signed for the orders, and cleaned both the kitchen and the dining room. In the evening, usually after eight, she dragged herself to the back door to wait for her mother or Elnora to take her home, only to begin the routine again the next morning.

Contrary to what Marge Jones had told her, the woman took no real interest in the restaurant. G. Carter spent more time in the kitchen than Lena had been led to believe. Both Elnora and Aggie had told Lena not to expect much from Old Lady Jones because she was lazy. Not that she wasn't an okay white woman; she was just lazy and spent most of her time wallowing around smoking and watching television. Most of the time, Lena found out, she was back in the room off from the kitchen asleep on the cot as the TV played. G. Carter, on the other hand, was always somewhere around, underfoot, in the way, keeping an eye on how much money came in and how much food went out. With piercing green eyes and dark hair, he was a tall man who wasn't too bad to look at, but Lena didn't trust him because she sensed he was sneaky. Then she was sure of it when Elnora and her mother pulled Lena aside and told her that the woman caught in the motel room was white, but the man was G. Carter, and he couldn't be trusted any further than she could see him. Mrs. Jones had kicked the woman off the place, but she had simply thrown up her hands at G. Carter. "Poor Marge Jones," her mother and aunt said to her. "She lets that man treat her just like a dog." His feelings about colored women, Elnora and her mother couldn't be certain. "But one thing for sure," Elnora told Lena, "me and your Mama got our eyes on him cause we don't want to have to kill him."

Lena wasn't afraid of G. Carter Jones. He was just a terrible inconvenience to her. Always in the way, like a mangy cat or a whining dog. With all her other responsibilities, she had to keep an eye on him. At times he would be in the kitchen checking behind her after she filled out the stock orders, and he always made some comment about what she had on or how she smelled and asking questions about her husband, the children, and whether or not she planned to have others.

One day after the restaurant had closed and Lena was putting away the mop and bucket, he tipped into the kitchen like a cat. Closing the door to the room where Marge lay sleeping, he grabbed the mop from Lena and smiled kindly. "Why don't you set down for a spell. I know you got to be tired with that crew that just left."

There had been several men who had begun a job on the highway and they ate their mid-day and evening meal at the restaurant. They had been particularly ornery this evening, snapping their fingers and yelling out the orders, complaining about the food, and all the while eating like stray dogs. For a fleeting moment, she had thought about quitting.

Lena wiped her hands on her apron and reached for her purse on top of the storage freezer. The smell of cooked onions from the afternoon meal still hung in the air. "I'll be going now. Elnora picking me up today."

Sweat beaded on his forehead and wiping it with the back of his hand, he took a long breath. He stood as if he were trying to figure out what task to take on next. "I could've took you home this evening," he said. "I ain't got nothing else to do."

"Well, thank you just the same, Mr. Jones, but Elnora waiting for me." She suddenly sensed his inching closer and she felt caged in. He smelled like a dusty room and Lena turned toward the back door.

"You ain't got nothing to be scared of," he said, as if he had been misunderstood.

"I ain't scared," Lena said and walked past him. "It's just time for me to go."

"I just want you to know how much I, I mean we, 'preciate what you do here." Folding his arms across his chest, he glanced quickly toward the closed door. "I know Mrs. Jones ain't been much help, but she feel the same way I do." His eyes followed her to the door. "Why, she always speaking highly of you."

"If y'all think so much of me, how come I still make $15 a week, Mr. Jones?" Lena reached for the outside door. She was tired, drained from the afternoon crew, and she didn't feel like any of G. Carter's deceitful conversation.

G. Carter reached toward her shoulder, but then dropped his hand. "It wouldn't take much for me to give you a little raise," he said, almost pleadingly. "I could give you twice the money you making if . . ."

"If I what?" She shot back.

He lowered his eyes toward the floor and clasped his hands in front of him. "I'm sorry. I didn't mean to. . . I didn't mean no harm."

Memories of every raggedy-behind white man she had ever worked for rose before Lena as she shoved her way past G. Carter and out the door. Every one she had ever challenged for cheating her mother, those she had argued with for following behind her brothers to make sure they were working, the ones she subconsciously killed for humiliating her husband every time he went out looking for a job—G. Carter, even in his uncertain behavior, was every one of these men. She wasn't slaving on the farm, but she was slaving just the same. She had fought hard to keep pessimism out of her mind and heart, but it was hard not to wonder if colored folks were just doomed to be forever at the mercy of white folks. Well, she said to herself, she'd be damned if she was going to put up with any of G. Carter's foolishness, on top of all the other things she had come to hate about the job.

And the thing she hated most, even more than the way G. Carter always seemed to be sneaking around like some old hungry hound dog, was the way she had to hand colored folks their food orders through a tiny window to the outside of the cafe, when whites came in and sat down to be served. Whites, even those who wandered up and down Highway 29 picking up trash, sat down at the table as if they owned the place, and colored came up to the window, pecked on it like an escaped slave, and mumbled their order. They had done this for so long, that they did it as naturally as washing their hands or brushing their teeth. Each time Lena packed a bag and handed it through the tiny window, she felt as if she were a co-conspirator in this ugly thing she couldn't define.

One day, after she had been working at the restaurant for almost six months, a car with New Jersey license plates pulled up into the lot of the motel. Through the window, Lena watched three men, two women and a small child get out of the car and start toward the dining room door. Mrs. Jones was in the back watching television and G. Carter had gone into town. Lena heard the door spring back, and figured the people must have been in the restaurant. She knew there were only two customers in the dining room, regulars from the neighboring rock quarry, and she felt nervous, almost scared. Glancing quickly back toward Mrs. Jones, Lena reached up for the ordering pad. Her palms were sweaty and suddenly she felt a rush, but this was going to be one time colored were going to get the

same treatment as whites.

"What will y'all have this morning?" Trying to calm herself, she looked up at the clock on the wall. "Oh, it's ten after twelve. Dinner time."

"Dinner? You eat dinner this early? We eat lunch this time of the day." One of the women smiled warmly. Tall, thin and dark, she reminded Lena of a young Elnora.

"Well," one of the men said. "Down here, they call it 'dinner,' and they call 'dinner' 'supper.'" He reared back in his chair authoritatively and looked at Lena out of the corner of his eye.

"How you know?" The other woman asked. "Just cause you lived here a thousand years ago, don't mean nothing."

The man winked. "They ain't changed," he said and snickered. "Well, I take that back. They made one big change."

The others looked at him with questioning eyes.

"We setting here, ain't we? It's 19 and 59, and we setting right here in this here restaurant in Rockingham County, North Ca-ro-li-na." He leaned his face toward the little boy, who made faces in his glass.

They all laughed.

One of the other men raised his eyes at them and said, "Come on ya'll, we taking up the woman's time."

Lena's eyes shifted toward the two white men as though they shared some common knowledge. They were looking from her table to her, and Lena looked back at her guests. "I can come back if you want me to." She thought if she went back into the kitchen, she might calm herself and pray that the white men would leave without causing any trouble.

"Naw," one of the women said. "We ready."

As they started to order, Lena could feel the sweat forming between her fingers. Her hands were trembling so she could barely write. Just as the little boy began to order, Lena saw one of the white men come toward the table.

"And I want . . . I want a big . . ." He raised his hands and made a circle with his thumbs and index fingers.

"Lena, what you think you doing?" the white man interrupted.

Lena looked squarely in the grey eyes of the lanky white man. "What do it look like? I'm taking a order." Her voice was firm, but she squeezed the pad to steady her hands. "Something I can get for you?"

The white man took off his cap and smoothed the thin brown hair from his forehead. "I bet Mr. Jones don't know nothing 'bout this."

The people looked anxiously from the white man to Lena. "Is something the matter?" One of the women asked.

"No," Lena said and then looked at the white man. "If there's nothing you want, then I'll take your money soon as I get through here." She turned back to the little boy. "Now, what was that, sugar? I'm sorry."

"Come on, Henry," the white man yelled. "I done lost my appetite eating in the same room with these here niggers. Mr. Jones going to hear bout this, and your black ass going to be out of a job." He pointed his finger back at Lena as he started toward the door. "We ain't paying neither, and you tell them why."

The three men from New Jersey had stood up while the white man yelled at Lena. Their eyes following the white men as they moved toward the door, they stood together forming a shield between the white men and Lena. "We didn't mean to cause you no trouble and we don't intend to let nothing happen to you," one of them said. "Least not while we in here."

"We just took a chance coming in here," the other one said as they each moved back to the chair. "I was just hoping things had changed."

Lena frowned. "That's all right. You ain't caused a bit of trouble. Just enjoy your dinner . . . I mean lunch." She laughed, relaxing the lines in her forehead.

"We can go if this cause trouble," the woman said, looking more like Elnora.

"No, Ma'am. You'll do no sucha thing. It'll be all right."

While the people ate their dinner, Lena paced the kitchen floor. Every now and then she peeked in the dining room to see if anyone else had come in, but she kept one eye on the door to Mrs. Jones' room just in case the woman came stumbling out into the kitchen. Lord knows, she didn't need Mrs. Jones coming out, dipping into the pots and licking spoons, then turning around and staring in the faces of colored people.

When Lena had finally gotten tired of straining her ears to get some clue to what was happening in the dining room and the back room, she decided to go check on her customers. The little boy was finishing his water and wrapping his burger in his napkin, while the others were impatiently watching him.

"Can I get y'all anything else?" she asked, clenching her pad in her hand. She didn't want to rush them, but God, she wished they wouldn't still be here when G. Carter returned.

"Naw, I don't know 'bout everybody else, but I'm full as a tick, and I betcha I'll be sleep fore we get to town," the man said. "You a mighty good cook. Ain't nothing like that good ole down home cooking." He chuckled as he rubbed his stomach.

"Pay the woman," one of the other man demanded. "How much we owe you, Miz?"

Quickly, Lena wrote out the bill, tore it off the pad, and handed it to the man who had done most of the talking. He glanced at it, and commented on how much such a meal would have cost up north. Fingering in his back pocket for what Lena thought was his wallet, he pulled out a thick wad of bills and peeled off two 20 dollar bills. "These ole rebbish crackers ain't changed a lick," he said. "They act like them kids in Greensboro ain't raising a stink bout this shit."

They tipped Lena twelve dollars and thirty-two cents, more than half of the amount she had collected during the last two months she had been working at the restaurant. By the time she looked up from the crumpled bills, the people were outside the door. "Y'all come back," she yelled, raising her hands. "And thank you. I sure 'preciate this." With her voice trailing, she waved the bills in the air and smiled. "Thank you," she said to herself. "Thank you." She looked down at the money, thinking about what the man had said about the people in Greensboro and remembered that she had seen something on Mrs. Jones' TV about a sit-in at Woolworth's. Oh well, she mumbled, as she watched the car out of sight, "I don't have time for no daydreaming. G. Carter be back shortly."

When they had gone, Lena breathed a sigh of relief. She had done it, and nothing had happened. At least, nothing important. What's more, she felt good about it. All this foolishness about colored folks coming to the side of the window like some dog begging for scraps. It didn't make a lick of sense. Who started this foolishness, anyway, she wondered as she swept the dining room. It ain't nothing but slavery time stuff, and I ain't no slave.

Lena had finished cleaning the dining room and washing all the dishes when Mrs. Jones came out of her room. With puffy eyes and a sour breath, her face was red and swollen and her overly-teased hair was mashed to her head on one side. When she came out, she left the door opened, leaving the T. V. in full view.

> ...her face was red and swollen and her overly-teased hair was mashed to her head on one side.

"Whyn't you go on in there and set down for a spell. I know you tired. Ain't going to hurt nothing. Then you can look without stretching your neck out its socket." The woman laughed.

Lena could hear Mrs. Jones laugh over the laughter from the TV as the woman walked heavily into the kitchen. She didn't know what was louder—Mrs. Jones' bare feet slopping against the linoleum, the TV or her heart pounding. The realization of what she had done was scary, but if she had to do it over, she'd do the same thing. She took a deep breath. "Thank you, Jesus," she mumbled. "Thank you, Jesus."

"What you looking at?" Mrs. Jones yelled back at Lena.

Lena rested her chin on her hands. "'What's My Line', I believe."

Gnawing on a chicken leg, Mrs. Jones came back into the room, sat down on the cot, and crossed her plump legs. "You want to watch that?"

"I guess it's all right. I'll be going home in a little while. Soon as Elnora get here." Lena cut her eyes at the woman and watched her pull on the chicken bone.

An empty bottle of Old Taylor lay on the floor next to the cot, and Mrs. Jones reached over and clutched the neck of the bottle. With her lips quivering, she leaned her head back and drained the bottle. "Git this little corner here. Can't let none of this go to waste."

The laughter from the TV now sounded like a distant echo while Mrs. Jones continued to talk. Lena tried to watch the people guess what the little baldhead man did, but not even Gary Moore had any ideas.

"You don't drank none of this stuff, do you?"

"No Ma'am." Watching Mrs. Jones, Lena's mind wandered to the people from New Jersey and then all the colored people who had pecked on the window to the kitchen. It just wasn't fair.

"Well, good for you. And may you never have cause to take a little drank, cause chile, this stuff'll git a hold of you and turn you every which way but loose." She propped an unsteady head in her hands. "But this some good stuff, girl. Ain't nothing like a little swig to git you up when things is down." Resting a ham hand on Lena's shoulder, she tilted the bottle and looked into it. "All gone, look like." She cut her eye sharply at Lena. "You know why I do this, girl?"

Lena cleared her throat to keep from answering. Yes, she wanted to say. I know. You lonesome. You lazy, you got a husband that treat you like trash, and you don't have nothing better to do. She kept her eyes focused on the T. V.

"You think I got it made, don't you? Bet you wish you was me, hunh?" Mrs. Jones clutched the empty bottle toward her chest. "Well, girlie, I could tell you a thing or two." She became silent, her eyes distant. "Sometimes, I wake up in the morning and I just dread to see daylight. I say to myself, "If I pull the cover over my head, it'll still be dark, and I won't have to face the day. But then I hear G. Carter stumbling around out yonder," she pointed to the kitchen, "and I know the day is here." She dropped her hand, letting it rest on Lena's arm.

Mrs. Jones' voice was no longer hard and scratchy like a radio with too much static. But now, Lena thought, it was weak and thin, almost like a lost child. Lena felt the pressure of Mrs. Jones' cushy hand on her arm and noticed the moisture settling in the deep fleshy craters under her eyes.

"It just ain't easy," she said, her voluminous chest rising and falling with each breath. "It's like trying to run, ankle-deep in mud."

For a few minutes, the only sound was the laughter from the TV. The panelists were still trying to guess the bald-headed man's profession.

Suddenly, Mrs. Jones jumped up. "I'm sorry," she snapped, wiping her eyes with the back of her hands. "I got to make me a little run." She snatched her purse from the top of the television and ran out the door. "Be back in a few minutes. If Mr. Jones git back fore I do," she yelled from the kitchen. "Tell him I ain't gone far."

"I hope I'm gone," she mumbled, feeling the tension easing from her body like an old habit. She turned back to the television. The panelists were looking around at each other and laughing like they had gone mad. The bald-headed man grinned unwittingly, his head turning from the host to the panelists like a dummy. Lena had missed the part of the show where Arlene Dahl guessed what the man did, but the host was still talking about it. The guest was a monkey trainer.

Illustration by Laura Kogonis

Illustration by Laura Kogonis

A Year on the Floor: Journals
Robert Gregory

keywords: love, assholes, gluttony, empty, pride, envy, people you can't see

After the rush, we were all leaning on the counter, waiting for action from the last few tables. Christine told the story of her suicide: during some desperate phone call, "Do you care if I die?" she said to her daughter and her daughter said "No!" and hung up on her. So she took a lot of Tuenols and Valiums, already had speed in her and hundred proof vodka. This guy "Jewish, a social worker type, I think he was interested in me, I wasn't interested in him at all, how could somebody have been interested in me then?" called her up when she was far gone and when he heard what she was doing, came rushing over. He and Christine's brother broke into the house and carried her out. On the way to the car, they dropped her, so she had a black eye and bruises when she got to the hospital. She laughed at this picture of herself.

She woke in intensive care. "I opened my eyes and my father was there, crying. I guess he didn't know what to do...He gave me his watch." She laughed. "This big expensive watch. Then, when I was okay, about a week later, he asked for his watch back!" She laughed again. Christine has big luminous eyes and the loudest laugh of anyone in the restaurant. She often laughs at her own stories, especially the sad ones.

Four old hags appeared at the door. "Oh dear," George says, "They probably want a booth." He has the booths today. He had been hoping for decent money and old ladies are notoriously bad tippers. Any woman was, old or young, unless she'd been a waitress herself. In fact, the tip might be bad just because there was one woman in the party. Wives sneak back to the table and pocket part or even all of the tip once the husband is out of range. You had to rush over and grab it but the really experienced wives knew to snatch it up quickly in a practiced movement as they were leaving the table.

Once, Alice said, she managed to collect her tip, all of it. Then she heard "Yoohoo!" She was being summoned by the wife, who had hung back on some pretense.

"Don't you think that's too much tip money for lunch?" the lady asked her.

Alice (defiantly): "No."

Lady: "From a woman?"

Alice (the wife of a man in the seminary training to be a missionary) had to tell the truth: "Well, yes."

And so she ended up with half of what he gave her.

A quavery old voice nearby cried, "Sir! Sir!" Sir always meant trouble. The old woman was holding up a partly eaten object. "This matzo ball," she said, her eyes bulging with indignation, "is cold!"

On my way past the salad bar into the kitchen I saw Diane filling a teapot and passed on the message: "The old whore at 37 told me her matzo ball is frozen solid."

"Oh, why doesn't she choke on it, the old bitch?" Diane said as she raced past.

Push through the swinging door out of the dark and cool dining room, the soft low light and conversation, into the hot, dirty, loud zone. Flames leaping from the stovetops, clouds of steam from the dishwasher. Along the steamtable soups and sauces in big rectangular tins steamed and bubbled. Underfoot crushed lemons, scraps of ragged lettuce, smears of blackening catsup. Every surface shining with grease. Two radios blasting from either end of the line -- one on the white station, one on the black station. Cooks yelling orders, shouting insults to each other and curses at the waitresses, the waitresses screeching back over the radios and the curses, trying to find out what had happened to their orders. All in a hard bright light, doubled by the white of the cooks' uniforms, doubled again by the stainless steel counters and shelves.

> **Every surface shining with grease.**

Frank telling me gravely: "You've got to make the breakthrough to handling five tables at once." Which is true, since that is the only way I'll make enough money to stay alive on. Five at once means a whole section seated at the same time, which means good turnover; with luck (the cooks don't screw up, I don't screw up, the people are good-humored) I can manage about $900 a month. Just enough.

Jack out here doing salads, saying to Lucy: "The Professor's the coolest waiter we got." He meant that I never spazzed. This wasn't true. The waitresses standing there loudly disputed this, telling him how angry I would get sometimes, throwing trays, cursing people, dumping meals into the garbage instead of delivering them. Jack shook his head, just thought they were being female and disagreeing with him automatically.

Ozzie is the one who invented the name "Professor." "Where's that chicken romano special order, Oz?" I'd shout, way behind and in a big hurry in the early days.

"Hey, you're the professor, you tell me!"

While they were working side by side doing pancakes and omelets Ozzie made a sign and stuck it on Jack's back: "Kick me. I am a asshole."

"Ozzie," Jack said, when he found it, "you dumb ass, not a asshole, an asshole. Isn't that right, professor?" I told Jack he was correct. Ozzie looked strangely abashed.

Trout on the menu. The fishheads were removed, but for some reason they were left out on a white plate in the kitchen, their gaping mouths and fixed dead eyes a treat for Andy who thought they were hilarious. He put one in Beth's pocket for her to find later when she reached in for her cash. Later he put one in his mouth, as if he'd just swallowed the rest of the fish. He said to Diane as he loaded her tray, "Ask them if they want head with their meal." "Oh, grow up," she said, swaying past with a big tray on her shoulder.

Pompous young guys, who order for their date: "and the lady will have " while the woman sits there silent and apparently appreciative. I always sneak a look at the women but they never seem to have any look of boredom or secret amusement at this rigmarole.

Timing and memory. Also balance. I maneuver, loaded tray high on my shoulder, through milling crowds of customers and waiters. "Behind you," I've learned to say, to warn people I am right there. "Behind you."

Another kind of balance: I can't afford to get ruffled or sulky when people are rude or annoying. It slows me down too much and ruins my tips. Not that I couldn't lose a tip now and then for the sake of dignity but the managers notice and if you seem calm and cheerful they give you the good sections, the busy ones, where you can make a living if you don't spaz too much. They don't have to fire anybody, just give them slow sections and pretty soon they aren't able to pay the rent.

Judy brought a cheesesteak back into the kitchen because the customer had complained, "not enough meat." Andy got a smaller roll and dug the meat out with his fingers and stuffed it in to the new little roll, so it would look like more. Judy objected in her grave way and Andy, amused, told her, "Hey, it's all customer perception."

By the end of a busy night, our hands have cuts and burns, and our uniforms and shirts and especially shoes get covered with traces of garbage: smears and splashes of dropped food, thrown food, halfeaten food, garbage (especially Russian dressing and catsup, which gets on you somehow even if no one ordered it all night).

Sometimes people ask me about teaching since it seems to them a nice life. My answers don't help. I don't understand it myself. Once Christine and I were by ourselves in the peaceful time before the restaurant opens, putting the chairs down and setting the tables. She asked me about it and I told her (it suddenly came to me) that I finally realized I had read all the great wisdom of the Western world and I was still just an asshole.

She laughed. Then she said, "Are you getting less of an asshole doing this shit?"

I stopped, fork in hand, to consider it. "Maybe," I said.

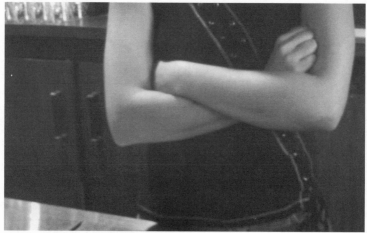

© 2003 Karen Ocker

A woman grilled me, suspicious about my claim that the cappuccino machine was broken. "It's been broken for years," Christine once told me. "And if they ever fix it, I'll break it again, personally. Pain in the ass bullshit."

Then the customer said, as if I had already cheated her hundreds of times, "Well, bring me a piece of that chocolate cake then if it's fresh! if it isn't fresh, don't bother." Then the four-top. One old lady, peremptory: "Hot Fudge Sundae with the hot fudge on the side" and then when I brought it, "Is this all the whipped cream I get! What, you running out of whipped cream! Look at this!"

At another one, "You make your shakes thick here? I want it thick." Randy was on desserts. I told him, "Make it thick for the fat lady." He grinned and said, "Bring her over here, I'll make it thick for her." The fathers all disgusted, the mothers all starved and suspicious.

A slow day shift. Deitrich proposed a philosophical question: when a fly comes in to land upside down on the ceiling, does it do a loop or just roll over? For a while we watched them carefully. But no matter how many times we saw the fly land, we couldn't be sure just how it did its trick.

Double shift today. Very busy. My head bloated and full of warm jelly (I have a cold). Christine made me hot water with lemon and honey and insisted I drink more when I got home. She stole three lemons for me from the kitchen and put them in my knapsack.

She told me a story: "I had just been beaten up by this guy, and I was sitting in an empty parking lot in my car, over near La Normande, the fancy French restaurant, thinking how much I hated this guy. Of course I was high and probably drunk on vodka too. These two guys saw I was alone and decided to rob me. The car doors were unlocked so they climbed in, one in back and one in front, and talked to me -- probably to keep me from screaming while they went through the stuff in the car. But I was so out of it I wasn't even frightened. I was glad to have someone to talk to (she laughed). So I just began telling them my problems with this guy and then my problems in general. Meanwhile they found all these weird things when they went through my purse, no money, no credit cards, but little toys and photographs and bits of stuff, mystery junk, the cuckoo clock I kept in the back seat, so they changed their minds and decided to leave me alone. One of them said, as they were leaving: 'Don't worry, everything will turn out all right.'" She laughed at these two robbers trying to encourage her to look on the bright side.

Luther is about sixty, big and round. The guy who drives the supply truck calls him "Sasquatch." He doesn't care. He likes size. He likes the waitresses if their hips are wide and their asses big and round. "Elizabeth Taylor, now, she looks good," he confided one day and then he giggled. His voice is normally low, but when something tickles him, he has a little highpitched giggle like a small delighted girl. Sometimes he and Jack open but more often he and Ozzie are in early to set up, Ozzie in the empty kitchen and Luther out in the empty dining room in the dark, vacuuming in a forest of upturned chairs.

We are working and tired and bored and sick of it while they are at their leisure and get to be infantile and demanding. Envy.

Maryann said her boyfriend and his buddy were both drunk on Jack Daniels when she got home last night. She didn't feel like dealing with two drunken assholes at that time of night so she told the guy it was time to leave. He just sat there, blitzed and dazed. So Maryann, being a big strong woman and feeling exasperated at this welcome home, dragged the guy bodily out of the apartment. "I was going to walk him down the stairs but I lost hold of him on the landing. He fell down the stairs and then hit his head crack on the door." Outcry from the listeners.

"I checked him," Maryann the physical therapist in training said calmly. "His pupils were normal."

Christine said she got a baby chick for Easter one year when she was a kid. She named it "Lucky," and it lived outside in the shrubs. She loved it intensely and it loved her. It would wait with the crossing guard for her to come home from school. Eventually it grew larger, got a crop, and started to crow so she had to give it away to relatives who had a farm. "And when I went there a month later, Lucky didn't recognize me and I didn't recognize Lucky!" She laughed.

Luther asked me if I had any kids and when I said no he told me that he had a son who was in prison. He said it very calmly. Said the boy's grandmother must have spent $20,000 getting him out of jail over and over and every time he goes right back in again. "I guess he likes it, he keeps on going back there."

Tonight Christine said to do this stuff you need to be empty. She meant (I think) empty of your own concerns, empty of needs, transparent. I don't know for sure because we only had a second and then we raced off to finish our ordering. I heard Darryl's voice from the kitchen: "Y'all are creeps -- creep motherfuckers!" because he wanted to get done fast and go to some party but more dirty dishes kept coming in at him.

Yesterday Ricki saw the new waitress -- Tina -- and said, "Oh no, is she working here now? She's such a slut! When I worked at Eat'n'Park with her she used to go in the kitchen and say, 'Hey guys, want to see my new underwear?' and lift her skirt up, 'Nice, huh?' She finally got married to this guy and he'd tell me, 'She stays with me because I'm the best she ever had. But she cheats on me because I don't have a car.'

He'd tell me all this stuff! I didn't want to hear it. I mean "

Tina's tiny so she makes a loaded tray look huge. She's tight-faced and eager to please so she makes a lot of mistakes. Crazy John the dishwasher, in a rage again, shouts: "Don't put them forks in there, you dumb bitch!" He terrifies her. He's wet with sweat and spray from the washer, hands glittering with white people's grease. Upstairs in the men's room (smell of a urinal full of cigarettes and dark yellow smelly pee) he showed me the tape across his belly muscles.

"Dude cut me, man. I don't feel too good tonight, you know?"

"John," Jack said in a shocked voice, "what'd you do?"

"I don't let nobody disrespect me, man," he said. "Nobody." We're side by side catching a quick drag in a rapid second before we run back down. Noise and shouts come up from the kitchen, as if there's a battle going on. He looks dizzy and in fact he staggers a little when he starts back down.

Tina puts her mascara on thick. She talks in a rush, worried about the manager:

"HehatesmeIknowhedoes."

"He hates everybody," I say, to cheer her up. "Don't worry about him." But she's one of those people who give off a signal: scare me, hurt me -- and when they do, she runs faster, gets clumsy, drops a glass, gets more crazy. The jagged fragments on the floor look . . . interesting. "Get back to your tables!" the manager snaps suddenly right behind her and she scuttles away. He pushes open the door into the kitchen and says, "John, get a broom." John looks like someone should sweep him up and throw him away his eyes at least, but someone wants water, so I miss the rest.

A week later she was gone and John was gone soon after.

Christine talked about people who knew her in her old life, when she was an addict. Rehab counselors, cops, dealers. Sometimes they walk in here and she has to wait on them, which she hates.

The Ice Tea Man appears at the door. Who's going to get him? He always hopes it will be a waitress rather than a waiter, so he can ask her an innocent question or two, get into a conversation, maybe get the conversation going long enough to ask her out, although of course she'll say no, but at least he can look at her meanwhile, watch her hands as she sets things down in front of him, her hair, her eyes, her throat, because young women don't come close to him except in situations like this.

Ice Tea Man is doughy and puffy. His clothes and

his face look rumpled, as if he wandered in here right from bed. His inky hair is mashed down and greasy, his round cheeks dotted with black spikes of beard.

He comes in daily, sometimes twice daily, to sit and smoke long menthol cigarettes in his own peculiar way, with jerky, abrupt movements and shivers. As if the cigarette kept trying to get away from him and he had to snatch it back to his mouth.

He looks lonesome and sad. But to a worker in the so-called service economy, that's irrelevant: he is extra trouble and no tip, an occupier of valuable table space.

Tonight as I stood leaning on the salad counter waiting sleepily for a table of drunks to order their desserts, I glanced over just in time to catch Jack in the kitchen spin his big floppy white hat up into the air the way he spins pizza dough, so that it rose gracefully, spread out, then came down perfectly onto his head again. He saw me watching and we grinned at each other.

At one of my tables, a young boy dining with his mother who smelled so nicely of perfume. She asked, "Do you have a small hot fudge sundae?" -- emphasizing the word "small."

"Yes, one scoop."

"No," the boy cut in. "Five scoops!"

On a sign from the mother, I brought him the small one, and to fake him out, the mother and his sister both said "Ah!" and "Ooh!" and "Look, they did give you five scoops!" and the boy was completely fooled by this and beamed gluttonously at his tiny hot fudge sundae as if it were a mountain. Customer perception.

When I came back later to bring them some water, he exclaimed in a delighted voice, "You have a magic restaurant!" His mother said, "He thinks that because he can't see the door from this angle. He thinks you go right through the wall."

"I do," I said. "Watch, I'll do it again" and I went back to the door and went through backwards, looking at him as I went, to enjoy his delight.

Frank the manager (somebody had said one time while we took forkfuls from a piece of stolen pie quickly at the side station) has a kid by some waitress.

"He likes them." Christine said. "Waitresses."

Today he stood by grinning while Ruth (one of the older waitresses) complained about her son. "He's fourteen!" she said. "Telling his buddy over the phone, 'I slipped her the tongue'!!" she says, indignant.

Frank says, "Slipped her the tongue where?"

She grins. "He don't need any new ideas, he's got plenty of them already."

Then she continues: "I told him how it works. 'I got pregnant with you and now I'll never be anything but a waitress the rest of my life. You say you love this girl. Is that what you want to do to her?'"

She paused and said: "Then he starts crying," sounding as if this surprised her. She made a face that said "I hadn't planned on telling him that but now he knows." It also said she hadn't said to herself until now that this was her story and would continue to be forever. Frank was still grinning at his interruption.

In the kitchen, "Hey, Prafessa," Ozzie yells, calling over the line in his goofy voice, "you get me what I want yet?" Each morning when I was new and worked days, I would say hi to him but he wouldn't answer or even look at me. Not until he thought up this joke. He's skinny and ugly, has that cook's skin, very white but not a clean white, a sweaty greasy white, like lard. Now he uses the joke to kid me about being here in this shitty job or halfkid me, since he also thinks I'm an asshole for doing it.

What he wants is pussy. "I gotta have some," he says, "I mean it."

"Watch this," he says, and sticks his tongue out as far as it will go. "Tell 'em I'll eat 'em all day and all night." He wags his tongue back and forth, puts on his best obscene grin. It looks more than obscene because he has pimples that never go away. He must have decided at some point: people think I'm ugly and stupid, okay, I'm not going to do them any favors and hide away.

Someone told me his wife is huge and mean. One day she threw him out of the house, either for gambling or out of jealousy. The other cooks made fun of him, which is attention he usually enjoys and giggles at but he was silent all that day.

Next day he seemed back to normal, on the back line pounding chicken breasts with a mallet: what the other cooks called "Ozzie beating his meat."

Arlene asked Jack if Ozzie and his wife were back together and he said, "Yeah. Why? 'Cause he loves her" pause "he loves an ugly bitch who hates him."

"Hey, Prafessa," Ozzie called when he saw me move past. He had found some pink and skinless meat with the right shape, held it up in front of his face and stuck his tongue through it, to show me his skills. Six months ago I would have thought this or that serious thing or just been embarrassed maybe. Now after all this time on the job I didn't think anything, just took a lemon from the bin and threw it at him. By good luck, it smacked him right in the middle of the forehead. He looked surprised, then smiled, dropped the meat, picked up a dirty rag and swung it like a batter warming up. So I pitched him more lemons, which he tried earnestly to hit. When he missed, they smacked the back wall with a satisfying sound and left a wet spot. After three strikes, he was out. He dropped the rag and went back to pounding breasts and I took off to deliver the coffee I was carrying. The transaction, whatever it was, was over.

Tonight Christine told stories about all the ways she used to try to get money from her family for drugs. She talked with regret about how much she tried her family's patience in those days. But she is embarrassed about her life now. She pays bills and stays sober and clean and nothing happens, nothing worth telling a story about. She said, "Now that I work as a waitress, they're overjoyed: 'That's wonderful!'" She scrunched up her face into an exaggerated grin of delight and patted her cheek to imitate them, then laughed, shaking her head.

Luther and I joke about the way he swipes bites of food, a chip here, a fry there. Whenever I go by, he's grubbin' (as the cooks say). Tonight he told me about a cousin he grew up with. "He got arrested and sent to this place like a juvenile hall. A mansion. Run by this old couple. They had a dog, a red bird dog and they told him his job'd be to feed the dog. Well, he got

Wheaties and milk for breakfast. But the dog got those linksausages, five of them, and scrambled eggs. And he ate veal chops, home fries. My cousin, all he got at home was beans, fatback. He told me, 'That dog was glad when I left. I ate his food every day.'" Luther laughed. "The owner asked him, 'How come the dog's not doing any loads in the yard?'" Luther laughed again, delighted at this question.

Later he asked me, "Lot of Communists out there tonight?" Instead of customers, he says Communists -- that's what he calls them in the joke he never gets tired of. Jack once told him, exasperated, "They ain't Communists, Luther!" Luther just smiled. He had been warned all through the Fifties about the enemy who would someday invade the country and take away all his freedoms and make him work like a dog. They were Communists all right.

Got off late last night, close to three, didn't get to bed till four am and so slept through the six am alarm woke up finally at seven-thirty (the alarm had rung the whole time) and had to rush to shower, put on cold wet socks I'd washed out last night, my only pair (I tried the iron and the oven to dry them but neither worked) and tramp out in the cold, spitting globs of yellowish stuff from this persistent cold. Waited half an hour for the 61C, my fingers and toes numb, my face raw and burning from the cold. Could feel my wet hair freezing to my skull, my brain freezing to the roots of my hair.

Tonight Ice Tea Man and an older woman with protruding eyes came in. He had a three days growth of black stubble and old stains where his belly pushed up inside his shirt. He wore a white jacket from a leisure suit to be dressy for her. He ordered "cheesesteak." Because of his lisp she heard "cheesecake" and exclaimed about that, "No, Willy, no cheesecake, it's not good for you, you're too heavy already!" He explained what'd he really said, irritated and embarrassed, and more so when she then said to me, "I don't want him to gain weight." His mother, it must be.

Later, as I passed them, I overheard him say, morosely, "Fat." She said, "Well, no, you're husky" and he immediately corrected her, "Fat."

Ricki was nearby eavesdropping and enjoying all this. She told me he asked her once if she had a boyfriend. She said quickly that she did and he said, "Is he alright?" She said she just stared, thinking to herself "alright?" and he said, "It's alright if he's not alright I mean I'm not alright myself."

Tonight Eddie is wearing a dime in his ear. Not outside, like an earring, but inside, like an earplug. When I ask him, he smiles the little smile and says, "Too noisy in here with that machine." It wasn't that at all, of course, it was to keep off witches (but

Illustration by Laura Kogonis

I didn't know that at the time and Eddie wouldn't be likely to tell me).

I used to hate the little smile. "Not only do I feel amused and superior," it said, "but I won't even bother to hide it." I saw it on people's faces as I trudged by on my way home, a load of books in my case, a load of trouble on my face. Why are they smiling the little smile at me? I wondered, paranoid and angry, probably talking to myself aloud. Fat, bearded like a furtrapper, eyes red and angry, fingers yellow with nicotine.

Now I like the little smile. I don't know why Eddie smiles it but there are a million possible reasons and anyway being a dishwasher and smiling is a rare combination. We get a new one every two weeks, it seems like. It takes a week to learn the job and a week to see it will never get any better. During that second week, they get angrier and angrier, more and more weary, and then they are gone. Eddie, so far, is still here, and maybe it's because of the little smile. Or maybe that's what he's smiling at.

Tonight Jane was telling me some trouble. She was always considering things before she said them but her boyfriend said whatever he thought, so he called her "evil" and "secretive." There had been a man she had really loved. He was older, she said. "He was perfect for me. I can get a little crazy and he could always make me feel peaceful. But I really want children and he didn't. He told me he'd had children already in his first marriage and he didn't want to go through it all again. But I really want children," she said, "so we had to break up finally." She looked down and away.

"Hey, Chief!" This from the old guy for whom nothing is hot enough—he waves his coffee cup. "I'll have that taken care of for you, sir." Through the swinging door into the roar and heat.

"Hey, Billy. Isn't hot enough."

Bill, mock-serious, says, "Here, I'll take care of it." Bends, puts it to his ass, farts, says "There" and then gives it back to me. I put it back on the tray and turn to take it out again but he starts laughing and shouts, "Wait, wait!"

He puts it in the microwave. "I'll give it five," he says. "That'll take the skin off his mouth."

Both today and yesterday I noticed a curious feeling of happiness and affection while I was at work. Every shout and instruction and tone of voice was familiar and understood, as was the sense of bustle and hurry when things got busy, the near-chaos, the repetitious movements of the people making a glass of iced tea or filling a cup of coffee or zooming by with a tray or arguing with a cook or gossiping while waiting for food to come up or a table to finish eating or the next table to be seated. This sense of the familiar is exactly the same element that I dislike: the repetition and boring routine.

The managers were talking about Luther the other day, explaining to some visitor that he can't read or write or add or subtract. "He just hands in the time card and we figure out his hours for him," Andy said. It sounded like he thought this was pretty hilarious.

Yesterday I worked a twelve. Christine told me about her mother's corpse. She used to tend to her as she lay in the living room, with tubes in her, and then one morning she died and Christine described being able to tell she was dead by touching her hand and having the most horrible feeling of being afraid. She said, "You know what it was, it was so quiet then, that's how you can tell, she was so still." She said she used to say later on when she was out high somewhere, "I have a wonderful surprise for you," and then take people out to the Jewish cemetery to see her mother's grave. She laughed at the weirdness of this. One time she was with two friends and they urged her on (she was afraid) to go to the grave itself. All of them went with her, high. They sat facing the grave under a blanket wrapped around all three of them and Christine told them stories about her mother and they told her stories about their mothers.

Saturday night I was trying to talk Christine into going back to school. To change the subject, she told me how much she hated her father when she was a kid. She and he fought with their fists while her mother lay in the living room dying of her heart condition. Her mother would drag herself up from the sofa and then fall down between them, pulling all the tubes loose. Christine said, "It was the only way to stop us fighting."

When her mother died, Christine was gone, maybe hospitalized or in jail, she didn't really remember, they moved all her mother's stuff up into the attic. One day much later on Christine went up there to look at her mother's things and found a Brownie camera with film still in it. She used up the film and when the roll came back from the developer, there was a picture of her mother, looking well and healthy. "It was like a gift of some kind, as if she deliberately left it behind for me because she knew how much I needed it," she said. She noticed two sweet little teadrinking ladies at her table beckoning to her and said in an undertone, "Oh, what the fuck do you want?" as she moved to them.

At one of my deuces, a young mother sat with her son who kept taking his toy hockey stick and whirling it around in the air. I went over to see if I could talk him out of that. When I got there she was telling her son not to swipe at the air with that stick. There were people in the air.

"People?" he said, surprised.

"You can't see them but they're there."

"What people are they?" he asked.

"The people you can't see," she said, and he laughed, surprised at her perfect child's logic. I burst out laughing too and she winked at me.

Christine told about her father and his 400-pound girlfriend. The woman wants him out but the father refuses to leave, so she calls Christine to come get him. "What else could I do?" Christine says. She goes over there and packs up his belongings for him: "pillowcases and trusses and Mylanta and laxatives." She laughs cheerfully at this. "What kind of romance is this?" she says. "He can't even get it up!"

On the back of a brunch menu, in red ink, a kid had drawn three Santas, all of them with savage glaring eyes and snarls.

Before work today I was sitting in Aiken's cafeteria across the street writing notes about last night when I saw through their glass wall that it had begun to snow. Just a few flakes at first, blowing past unnoticed by everyone, and then as I watched it grew thicker and the flakes were wilder and faster in their movements until the snow was all I could see, no more people, no more buildings or cars.

Illustration by Laura Kogonis

Coffee, Tea, No Bullshit
John Gelber with Leah Ryan

Q: What is your official title?

A: I guess I'm like the manager? (Laughs) Yeah, I'm sposeta be the manager.

Q: How long have you worked at the coffee shop?

A: Six years. I worked as a counter dude for most of that time.

Q: And now you're the manager/counter dude.

A: Yeah.

Q: So what did you like about the job when you first started?

A: It's coffee and tea and no bullshit. I loved the coffee…the raw beans, the roasted beans. I'd get the coffee oil all over me and I always smelled like coffee. Also, I met a lot of people. There's something about a coffee shop that's like a neutral zone. People can be real. The other thing is that the place is over 100 years old, so I was dealing with people who used to buy coffee there in the 1930s. They would tell me stuff about the coffee that the owner didn't have time to tell me.

Q: What's a bad day at the coffee shop like?

A: Customers call and complain their order isn't right, maybe a burner goes out, the afternoon guy calls in sick…but basically there's no such thing as a bad day.

Q: What about crazy customers?

A: We have a lot of mentally ill customers. Somebody else wouldn't even let them in the door. They're just looking for attention. We try to find out what they want and give it to them.

Q: They probably wouldn't get that much at Starbucks.

A: People just like Starbucks because they can go there and get their favorite frappalatta crap or whatever and it will taste the same in Cleveland as it does in New York.

Q: Have you noticed any changes in customers' attitudes in the past few years?

A: Lots of people are assholes just because they can be. Also, I've noticed that suburban people always want a "medium." There's something about choosing between a large and a small that they can't handle. So we just give them a small and tell them it's a medium and they're happy.

Q: Do you have any advice for coffee shop customers?

A: Yeah. Some people walk in the door and they start with a question. "Do you have Sweet'n'Low? Do you have this or that kind of tea?" Don't do that. Just tell me what you want. If you tell me you want a banana split, I won't be able to give it to you. But I can tell you where to get one. It's not about what we got; it's about what you want.

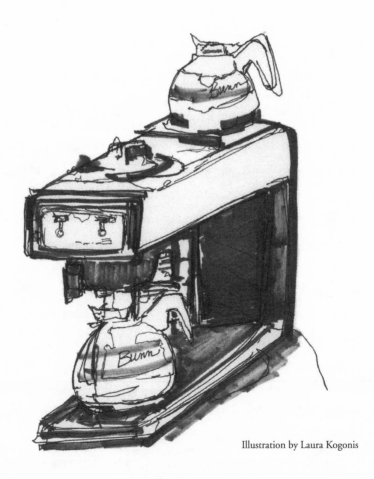

Illustration by Laura Kogonis

Jesus in a Saucepan
Matt Fedorko

I can't wash dishes anymore.

I haven't been able to for years.

Whenever I get near scalding water or wet cookware, my stomach turns and my hand hurts. I just can't do it.

I eat microwave dinners, mostly. They come in packages I can throw away easily. I buy the brand that sells the flavor separately and places it in an aisle I can never find. Not that I've tried.

I used to wash dishes professionally, if you could call it that. My rent was paid with the money from that wet, smelly job. This kid named Ricky and I worked together in the noisy recesses of a restaurant. He was a college dropout who used his shit pay to buy shit weed to get an even shittier high, and I was a college graduate who kept his diploma on his ceiling to remind himself that every day was supposed to be different because of that piece of paper. We knew what to do in the kitchen; we knew our way around. Ricky worked prep most of the time. He made salads, cut up vegetables, and portioned potatoes while I was ankle deep in dirty cups, plates, silverware, and slowly fading ideas about my future.

That future arrived, eventually, and now I scrape plastic food into my mouth with a plastic fork. At least I don't have to wash dishes anymore.

Sometimes, then, the plates wouldn't get clean. The silver would stay stained, and pots and pans just seemed to get greasier.

I hated those days.

When I had to run dishes through the tank three or four times, I would get tired quicker. I would be exhausted before the dinner rush. By the time I would get the bar glasses, smelling strongly of the alcohol saviors of so many of the bar's frequent patrons, I would be getting cold chills from the 120-degree steam.

I hated those days.

When I think about those days, one in particular, my hand still hurts. Sometimes I want to cry. Sometimes I do. No one sees me. I dry myself off afterwards. I wrap myself in large warm towels. I think, when I do, of Maria Rubo.

Maria found her Messiah staring back at her from her burrito in 1953. I saw it in a newspaper at the library. I saw the picture. I saw Maria's stony face, framed like a mug shot, with the burrito held tightly in front of her. I wonder what she was thinking when she saw it. I wonder what that burrito would've tasted like. And who would've done the dishes?
Maria Rubo probably crossed herself and uttered a prayer when her Mexican dish became a miracle.

So, when I saw Jesus looking hopefully past me, over my shoulder, from the center of a saucepan I had sent through four times, I wondered what was behind me and why this damn pan wouldn't come clean.

I wandered back to show Ricky. What else was there to do?

He was standing behind a long, smooth silver counter, slicing tomatoes. As I came closer, I watched him methodically remove the stem and put the whole tomato in the curved bay of the slicer. A second later, the tomato was gone, and he moved the slices that remained off to the side with the rest. I offered him the pan.

Ricky didn't even look up. I moved closer to show him the somewhat annoying miracle once again. Leaning forward, trying to place the pot between him and the tomatoes he was preparing to cut, I didn't realize I had also put my left hand under the efficient blades of the tomato slicer until Ricky's swift arm movement took most of it off.

No one paid attention to the pan as I slumped to the floor. Not the grill cooks who grabbed towels and rushed to my side, not the servers who ran for the phone, and not the manager who held my good hand tightly as if to say, "Don't die; you still have dishes to do."

> Don't die; you still have dishes to do.

I did, too. I had a lifetime of dishes, in one form or another.

Then, though, all I could feel was the oppressive wetness of my jeans. My legs felt crushed by them. All I wanted to do was change my pants and leave. Ricky could come too. We'd conquer the world, or at least get better jobs.

It may have happened, too, if I hadn't been bleeding so much.

My head fell to the side, ignorant to the hurried activities around me, and I saw that saucepan, rocking slowly back and forth on the floor. I could hear two words, faintly, spoken in time to its syncopated motions. Over the sound of splattering grease and the dinner rush, I could barely make out what the pan was saying. The cooks hoisted me up onto the table, peeling my wet pants from the slimy floor and shoving Ricky's tomatoes out of the way.

I looked as the saucepan tilted to the side one last time, paused, and fell back, silent. I pulled my manager close, inhaling deeply the scent of too much uneaten food that had held me for three years, and when I exhaled I carried those two words over my lips: "I quit."

No One Here Is Irish
Kristen-Hall Geisler

Sam checks herself in the mirror screwed to the back of her bedroom door: short black cotton-lycra skirt with a wide belt, orange underwire bikini top, and combat boots (should she need them). Nice tits, she thinks, fluffing them up a bit inside their holsters. She grabs the turquoise polo shirt with the O'Shaunessy's logo above the left breast off the bed, and heads out into the living room where Art waits, dressed in black pants and the royal blue O'Shaunessy's polo that all the kitchen guys wear.

"How do I look?"

"Nice tits." He grabs her bare waist and kisses her.

"I hope I make some fucking money for once."

"You will. If Doe-Eyed Girl can make money taking her shirt off, you can."

One of the lead servers is in the parking lot at the restaurant, telling everyone to park at the dentist's office up the road. Not only are they expecting a huge St. Patrick's Day crowd, being the premier faux-Irish chain restaurant in Tallahassee, but they've also cordoned off part of the parking lot as a beer garden. There's a white tent with rented tables underneath bearing tapped coolers full of green beer. There is a maze of orange plastic netting strewn around in front of the building, with one of the more muscle-y servers sitting on a stool at its head. He'll be the bouncer and ID checker when the real party starts in a couple of hours.

Inside, Art heads for the kitchen, and Sam heads for the manager's office. She takes off the polo and tosses it in the corner with some others. She takes $10 out of the filthy green apron she's tied around her waist.

"You ready to rock tonight?" Cory is grinning like an idiot, trying to get everyone excited about working on St. Patrick's Day. It's one of the biggest money makers for the restaurant -- besides football season -- and he stands to get a substantial bonus from corporate. He takes Sam's ten and hands her a commemorative St. Patrick's Day O'Shaunessy's T-shirt. Behind him, George, the other manager, rolls his eyes. George told Sam one time that having a psychology degree and being a restaurant manager means that you know precisely what kind of jerks you work with.

"Yeah, Cory. Ready to rock." She puts the shirt on and goes out to the floor. The idea is to buy the shirt from the restaurant for $10, then sell it off your back to drunken frat boys and lonely old men for as much money as you can get them to fork over. Last year, the female servers made hundreds of dollars; it's all they could talk about all week. The bartenders make bank, the cooks are tipped out like crazy, everyone rakes in the dough.

Three servers' sections of tables have been removed for a rented dance floor. Alec is setting up turntables, disk changers, and speakers. As the DJ, he doesn't have to wear any part of his uniform; he's wearing huge jeans and a New York Rangers jersey. People are slowly trickling in, checking out the setup, ambling to the raised bar in the center of the store. Most of the people at the bar are regulars, wanting to get in and out before the crush of college kids. In one corner is the guy who only drinks Murphy's Irish Stout from a proper British pint glass. Tonight he wears a tweed cap over his gray hair, a fisherman's sweater hanging from his shoulders, doing all he can to look like he just came in from Galway Bay. Hal, the local bigwig with the white toupee, sits at his tall bar table with his cronies. It's his table because it says so; there's a brass plaque with "Hal" etched in it bolted to the edge of the tabletop. In the darkest corner of the restaurant sit the Chivas Ladies, with their brass plaque on the wooden rail above the table. They're here so often O'Shaunessy's hired one of their daughters, despite the fact that said daughter has the IQ of a highball glass.

> For the early crowd, the managers have brought in a bagpipe band.

For the early crowd, the managers have brought in a bagpipe band. Five old guys in kilts and tasseled socks march around inside the restaurant, playing vaguely recognizable tunes. It apparently didn't dawn on the O'Shaunessy's brain trust that these folks are Scottish, not Irish. What does it matter at an "Irish" restaurant that serves fajitas and fried chicken salad.

After the bagpipers play a finale by the door, the rush of frat boys starts pouring in. Alec has been waiting for this, his cue, and turns up the music. Soon you can't walk from one end of the restaurant to the other without touching 40 or 50 people on your way by. Sam stands in the crowd near the front door, wondering how to get the strip show started. She decides to wait for the other girls to start. The guys will catch on and start asking her to take off her shirt. Then she can just haggle the price and go home with a couple hundred bucks at the end of the evening. It beats waiting tables. She's terrible at pretending to like people, and makes barely enough to cover her half of the rent.

"Hey! Can I buy one of those shirts!" A guy with his hat on backwards leans over to Sam's ear in order to be heard over the music.

"You can buy this one." Sam attempts coquetry, but it's hard to do when she has to yell. He steps back and looks at her, not sure what she's talking about.

"You can buy this one for $20. I'll take it off and give it to you," she explains.

"How much if I just buy one?" He is not getting the premise.

"You can't just buy one. You have to get it from me."

"All right." He digs in his wallet for twenty. Sam takes off her shirt and hands it to him.

"Thanks!" He moseys off in the direction of his friends. No appreciative glance. He seems a bit irritated that he has to buy a less-than-pristine T-shirt. She'll have to work on her sales pitch.

She spends another $10 for a T-shirt and heads back out to the floor. The Doe-Eyed Girl has a tray full of shots in cheap green plastic mugs on fluorescent orange cords. Where in the hell did she get that? She's talking to some guy, haggling over the price of her T-shirt, giggling and batting her eyes, so Sam takes a shot from the tray and belts it. She leaves the mug on the dark wooden railing that runs around the bar.

Sam walks up to the bar to see where these trays of shots are coming from. That would be an easier way to make money, with no conversation necessary. Just yell, "Two fifty!" at whoever wanted one, and the transaction would take place. The bartenders don't even notice her; one is lighting a woman's cigarette off his flaming fly. (A trick achieved with 151 and a lighter.) A guy pulls on Sam's sleeve.

"My friend wants to know how much for the shirt."

"Forty dollars." He bends away from her and toward his friend on the bar stool next to him, an older man with a white mustache. They are speaking French. Bolstered by the shot of whatever burning liquid she just drank, Sam steps in.

"You speak French?"

"He's from France," yells the younger guy. Sam wonders how long it'll be before he's puking on his Tommy Hilfiger sweater.

She works out, in French, that for $40 she'll take off her shirt and give it to Monsieur France. He smiles. "Oui! Oui!" He takes two crisp twenties from his wallet, and she takes off her shirt. She turns to go, but Tommy Hilfiger stops her.

"Can I take a picture?"

"Sure." Sam stands a few feet away, cocks one hip, and smiles. She feels fake, phony, and bored. Tommy Hilfiger sways as he moves in closer. He wants a picture of her tits. Sam doesn't care; they've been photographed hundreds of times; she also models nude for the art school. His hand shoots out with the one-shot quickness of a drunk and pulls at the center of her bikini. The flash illuminates the white skin of her breasts.

"Hey! What the fuck was that!"

"You took your shirt off." He sways back and leers, one elbow on the bar. It's her fault he's an asshole. Sam glances around her – no one else seems to notice what's going on, or care. Not even Monsieur France, who has turned back to watch the woman lighting her cigarette in this novel american way.

"Fuck you." She plants her right boot heel on the toe of his topsider, feeling the crunch of metatarsals under her foot. She spins on her heel, applying as much torque as possible, and walks back to the manager's office.

George is alone, not wanting to join what passes for revelry. "You want another one?" He reaches into a box for another T-shirt.

"No. I want a cigarette." She takes her uniform polo from the pile and goes out back by the dumpster. She tallies up her totals for the night: $40, a clumsy picture of her tits, a shot of unknown liquor, and the satisfaction of hearing an asshole's bones crunch. She knows it's not worth it as surely as she knows she'll be back again tomorrow, wearing this same shirt with this same yellow plastic nametag, smiling and serving.

Illustration by Laura Kogonis

Gunpowder Anniversary
Ra-Shime R. Rivers with Leah Ryan

Q: How long have you been driving a cab?

A: Two years.

Q: And how old are you?

A: Coming up on 29.

Q: How did you get into driving in the first place?

A: After high school I got a job at Jiffy Lube and became a manager. Then I got into an accident and was out of work for a while. Now I drive a cab part-time.

Q: Tell me about what happened a year ago.

A: It was a regular Friday night. Me and this other driver saw each other in the village (of Huntington, Long Island). I said hello, asked him how he was, and then I went back to the train station. Dispatch asked who wanted to go to the Carousel (a strip club) to pick up a regular (a dancer). Normally I would take that call. But this time the other driver took it. What happened was the dancer got in the cab, and they were followed. This guy who was following them wanted to kidnap the dancer. He ended up shooting them both. She grabbed the intercom and called the ambulance. I drove by and saw the scene, but I didn't know what had happened. I went back to the train station again.

Q: Were they both killed?

A: The driver was killed, and she was paralyzed. I hear she's walking again now, though.

Q: Did they catch the guy?

A: Yeah, they caught him a week later. He shot at an interracial couple, chasing them in his car. He got 30 to life. Turns out he did two other murders.

Q: How has this experience changed you?

A: At first I was too shocked to go back to work, but I had to go back. For one thing, that could have been me. Also it's the first time I've spoken to a person who was dead 10 minutes later.

Q: Is it still hard to go to work, a year later?

A: I hate it now. I don't do it as much as I used to. I do just enough to get by.

Diary of a Pizza Guy
Brendan Sullivan

August 20, 1999

When I drove up the second time, they were waiting at the bottom of the hill in accordance with their boarding school's rules. There was a time when I or any other pizza driver could meet them on campus, but that was not tonight. I almost felt bad for them having to wait on the edge of campus for a pizza, never knowing really when it would get there.

"Hey guys, thanks for waiting."

"What took you so long?"

I wanted to tell him how I came 20 minutes ago, like I said on the phone, and waited for them to show up. I wanted to tell him that because of his own prep school self-importance, my next delivery yelled at me for being late, and kept the tip. I wanted to tell him that no one seriously tied a sweater around their neck, and that it was just a joke that kids like me made about kids like him.

But I didn't. I was the pizza guy. My job was to drive and smile.

He handed me a crisp, clean fifty-dollar bill, and I prayed that I had enough change. It must have been after one of those three-day weekends when parents came to see school plays or soccer games and left money to ensure their child's education would not be hindered by the munchies.

He wanted all of the change.

With the amount these people spent on their kids' education, you would think someone could have taught them about tipping.

But I am the messenger, the only face involved in this process, and the only one to take anything out on.

October 3, 1999

Ring, Ring

"Pizza delivery, how can I help you?"

"Yeah, how many slices in a large?"

"Eight."

"How many in a medium?"

"Eight, same as the small and the large."

"Well if it's all the same, I'll just take the small."

> My job was to drive and smile.

October 14, 1999

When the phone rang that night, we were so closed that the trash from that day had already been picked up. I held up the receiver along with the last bite of the steamy spaghetti I had stayed late for. This was my shift meal, my consolation prize. It kept me busy while the boss's wife counted out my slips, minus my hourly wage, plus tips.

"Pizza Dewivewy, how can I help you?" I covered the mouthpiece and spat the too-hot noodles back on the plate, and soothed my mouth with grape soda.

"Yeah, can I get 50 pizzas delivered tomorrow to Worchester School?"

Nice, I thought, the boss is going to love this. I had no idea how he could ever make fifty pizzas in these two little ovens, but we needed the money. I heard a voice in the background and the sound of a car driving past.

"Hello?"

"Yeah, so, uh, Worchester School tomorrow."

"Okay, just plain cheese?"

Two other voices began to discuss the question before a hand smooshed over the mouthpiece on the other end of the line and muzzled all sounds. They really should have figured out what to get before ordering, I thought.

"Make that 25 cheese, 25 pepperoni." Man, I thought, those boarding school kids live it up. How much money does it cost to go to a school where they buy everyone pizza. What's more, the kid I delivered to at the school that day told me they were almost done with school and we in the town high school still had a month to go.

"Not a problem. Will you need any soda or chips to go with that?"

"No, can you bring them to the office of Stephenson Pikes?"

"We're really not supposed to come onto campus."

"Well he is the headmaster, so I am sure it would be okay."

Hey, who was I to argue with these guys? I had no idea what a headmaster was, but the name spoke authority.

"Okay, I'm sure you're right. Can you tell us which building to look for?"

"Yeah, right as you drive up, it will be the fourth building on your left as you come up the hill." I heard a car door slam, then a minor chortle. Then, click.

I hung up and I told the boss the good news. We all called him boss.

"That's a lotta pizza." He looked over the order ticket. Boss came to America seven years ago from Albania. For the first two years he bagged groceries and learned English at a Stop 'n' Shop down the street. Then he bought the pizza place, and his wife came out to join him. Since then, they were joined by two newborn babies, and both of their parents. The eight of them lived in a house on the edge of town.

Fifty pizzas was almost $500 coming in. That could buy new menus and tables or maybe get a display case to sell more pizza by the slice at lunch. Or maybe then we could get pizza lights for the top of our cars.

Of course, it was a much better idea to drive undetected. People always got nervous when they saw a pizza light heading toward them at above suburban speed. Usually they were the same people who complained when it took too long to get their pizza.

"What time they want it?" Boss squinted at the ticket, trying to read my handwriting and English. "25 L's X. 25 L's Pep. Stephenson Pikes, Worchester School."

I looked over the ticket, and discovered that he was right. Oh man, I hope I didn't screw this one up. "I'm sorry Boss, I'll call them back."

The number on the caller ID rang and rang. No answering machine. I tried it twice. This is why I should have left when I had the chance. Then Boss could have answered the phone and he would have remembered to ask all the questions.

"It's probably 12."

"But what if it is not? You could cost me a lotta business."

Boss asked very little of me. Answer the Phone, Speak English, Deliver the Pizza. Never once have I had to do dishes against my will, and both he and his wife insisted that I do my homework between deliveries. "Do your homework, go to school. Become doctor," they always said, "or lawyer."

"Who is this?" Boss pointed to the name at the bottom of the ticket. Of course -- the headmaster, I could just call him and ask him when to deliver. Even if he had left for the night, I was sure he would get the message early enough in the morning. I dialed the first four letters of his last name into the voice messaging system. Man, that school. Honestly, voice messaging?

"Hello this is Stephenson Pikes."

"Stephenson Pikes? My you're working late. This is Brendan from Pizzano's Delivery."

"Pizzano's?"

"Yes, I was just calling because I got your big 50-pizza order, but I forget to ask what time you wanted them delivered to your office." The unease I felt before during the whole ordeal before unraveled itself as I spelled out just what was going on.

He didn't even have to say it.

I'd been had.

That day, I thought about the kids up at the school in a whole different way.

They had always had a sort of attitude, one that doesn't care how long you waited for them.

But this was different. It wasn't them chanting "Hey, Hey, it's Okay / You Will Work For Us Someday," at hockey games. It was a blindspot that wouldn't allow them to see how costing a small pizza place hundreds of dollars was anything but a joke.

January 14, 2002

The car idled in the driveway of a trophy house mounted in the woods. I prayed my emergency brake would hold as I ran up the steps with the pizza. Years later I would pass this house and remember the order. Large Cheese, Large Pepperoni, two-liter Diet Coke.

This was not in a neighborhood known for its tips. This was in a neighborhood where the best I could hope for was to break even.

We didn't have cash registers in our cars, so when a pizza came out to $10.49, they either needed to have exact change or to round up. But on this street, I considered a deliver a success when I didn't have to spot them the 49 cents.

My usual act was to get them talking about working. You must be a hard worker to own a house like this, sir. Do you own your own business? Wow, you must be a hard worker.

This was a neighborhood of people born on third base who think they hit a triple.

Somewhere deep down the people in this neighborhood wanted to believe that everyone in the world made the same hourly wage, and that their riches were merely a product of late nights and overtime pay.

When presenting the pizza, I would stand outside in the cold on purpose to let the steam rise out of the bag.

Be careful there, it's hot. Can I put it down somewhere for you?

I want them to think that the box is so hot and fresh that only my hardworking hands can withstand the heat.

At the doorstep, I rehearsed three things I could say about their three story suburban palace. But before the doorbell could chime tonight, a woman in another room shouted, "I tell them every time to park on the street and walk around to the side door. Those idiots." A cupboard slammed and another voice scolded a screaming child.

People did weird things when they were hungry, and I figured that now would not be the right time to tell this woman that there is nothing remotely helpful about having Roman numerals for house numbers.

I wanted to tell her that I was sorry for the wait, but I only drive the pizzas, I don't make them.

I wanted to tell her that her screen door isn't soundproof.

When she came to the door, I put away the hostility and put on my pizza guy smile. "Hey, thanks for waiting. It's going to be twenty-three even."

"Listen, I tell them every time to park on the side street and come around to that door."

"Oh, I'm sorry. I've never delivered here before."

I satisfied myself by making comments to an imaginary co-driver. I'm sorry but we're not the fucking New York Times. We don't have a database that says where and how you like yours delivered.

Or

Maybe you could not tell by the rust pile idling in your driveway, but we have to cut out the luxuries in this job.

But again, I was nothing but smiles.

"Twenty-three even," I handed her the pizza. "Ooh, be careful, it's hot."

She handed me $25, which is a fairly appropriate tip. But then she asked for a dollar back. Now that hurt.

I wanted to say, thanks, I'll put this toward my third oil change this month, right after I get Rogaine for my bald tires. No really, a dollar is fine.

But, well, you get the picture.

A woman who looked like the one at the door walked up behind me. They must have been sisters or roommates, because they both yelled at an invisible child the same way.

"Sir?" she said.

This was the first time that was synonymous with my name, but it didn't carry any knightly respect. It felt more like when your mother used your full name to tell you what you had done.

"Sir? Is that your basketball in the backseat of your car?"

"Yes it is." I turned back to the woman at the door. "Okay, one dollar is your change, thank you very much." I turned to walk down the steps with my red, insulated pizza bag and my wide thank-you-for-your-order pizza smile.

"Are you sure that's your ball in the backseat of your car?"

The other woman leaned out the screen door and rested the pizza box on her hip. "What are you asking him?"

"I'm going to ask him again. Is that your basketball in the backseat of your car."

"Yes, that's mine."

"Are you sure? Are you sure you didn't just pick that up in our yard and put it in your backseat?"

This was worse than when she accused me of being late. Was there a formula? People who deliver pizzas later also steal children's toys?

"Excuse me?"

The screen door shut with the pizza and both women outside. "Why don't you answer her question?"

Now I carried only the pizza bag. "No, that is my basketball."

"Because my son has a basketball exactly like the one in the backseat of your car. Orange with black stripes."

I wanted to take back the box and say, my brother has a pizza exactly like this one: pie-cut and covered in cheese.

"Well, the one in the backseat is definitely mine." On the way home, I thought how I must have been in shock, because I thought of all the things I should have said. I should have told her that just because I deliver pizza, it doesn't mean I steal children's toys. I should have told her about her stupid Roman numerals.

Instead, I walked to my car and put the pizza bag back in the front seat. The woman followed behind and as I put on my seatbelt, she reached through my window, unlocked the back seat, opened the door, and pulled out my basketball.

At this point, would she even care if I told her how late they were making me for other people's pizzas?

She palmed the ball and squeezed it with both hands. "Hey, what are you—." I raised my voice, "Excuse me? I didn't say you—."

"Never mind," she shouted up to her sister, as she dunked the ball through my open car window and onto the passenger seat. "His is smaller."

The kid screamed again, because he was a kid. And the screen door slammed shut as I headed to my next delivery, late.

June 21, 2000

Ring, Ring.

"How many slices in a large?"

Here we go again, "Eight, same as the small and the medium."

Silence.

"Hello?"

"Wait ... how does that work?"

Years later, I got onto an elevator. I pressed the button for my dorm room on the fifth floor. The pizza guy next to me asked me to hit the button below mine for a delivery.

On the second floor, Ding, the door opened and a student walked in. He pushed the third floor button and stood against the elevator. He wore sporty nylon pants and his sweaty hair indicated that he had either just come from running or had just woken up. Either way his head hung sluggishly to the side.

I noticed the embroidered letter on his pants. "What's the 'W' for?"

He took off his sunglasses and looked at me. "It's for Worchester, it was the name of my boarding school."

"Oh no way, in Huborough?"

"Yeah."

"I grew up in that town."

He smiled through his half-glazed eyes, which were partially hidden under his intentionally filthy-white baseball hat. "Did you go to 'Chester?" Of course, his school had some cute, buddy-buddy nickname, the way people give brevity to local bars.

"Nah, I went to the high school, but I used to deliver pizza to Worchester."

"Oh really?" The door opened, and he stepped into the hallway. He looked both the pizza man and me up and down. "That sucks."

The door closed and I wanted to say something to him. I wanted to go back down to whatever floor he got off on and go over to him.

I wanted to tell him that the job did suck at times, and it was because of kids like him.

I wanted to tell him that I remembered him and that I spit in his food every time, even though I never did.

I wanted to tell him that maybe someday at a stuffy cocktail party someone will be impressed that he ran track at prep school, but for now let's leave the "'Chester" gear at home. I want to tell him Hey, Hey It's Okay/You'll Outgrow Those Pants Someday. Or Hey, Hey It's Okay/ I'll Drive Your Kids' Bus Someday.

But instead, I became a writer.

Illustration by Laura Kogonis

LIFE AT THE

CRACKED CRAB

I HIT TOWN DEAD BROKE. I FIGURED I'D START AT THE BOTTOM...

WITHIN 24 HOURS I HAD 2 DISHWASHING GIGS

WE LAMPIN' NOW

WHAT A SCORE

MY DAY GIG WAS AT A FAILING SEAFOOD JOINT ON THE ASS-END OF TOWN

FISH
CHIPS $4 95

DON, THE BOSS, WAS A KINDLY, INEFFECTUAL ALCOHOLIC OLD POOP

BILL, THE LEAD LINE COOK WAS A PUNK-ROCK PAROLEE AT LARGE

FROM A DRUG PROGRAM IN CALIFORNIA

THE WEED HE SCORED FROM HIS NAM-VET CRONIES GOT US THROUGH THE DAY

JUAN, THE SLEAZY PICK-UP ARTIST BARTENDER SOLD DILAUDIDS CHEAP

SOMETIMES I'D FIND THE WHOLE CREW OUT ON THE TILES

PIGEONS FLEW INTO THE HOOD VENTS TO DIE

(COO?)

RAIN MADE THE CEILING CAVE IN

THE MENU CHANGED DEPENDING ON WHICH PROVISIONERS WE COULD PAY

SPECIALS

~~CRAB~~
~~HADDOCK~~
VEG. SOUP

WE LEARNED TO SOAK ROTTEN FISH AND PRODUCE IN ASCORBIC ACID

TO RESTORE THE COLOR

THE HEALTH INSPECTOR SHOOK US DOWN FOR DRINKS

SHE WOULD GET SMASHED AND PASS US

Comic by Damian Carr

ONE MORNING I SHOWED UP TO FIND MYSELF LOCKED OUT

DON COULDN'T PAY THE ELECTRIC BILL

BUT HE WAS SURE AS HELL GOING TO PAY ME

I KNOW HE'S HOME

I TRACKED HIM DOWN AND GOT MY BACK PAY

LAST I KNEW DON WAS BARTENDING AT SOME GERMAN JOINT

HE WASN'T HAPPY

BILL WAS SQUATTING IN DETROIT

THE SKINS KICKED HIS TEETH OUT

JUAN WAS SELLING OFFICE PRODUCTS OUT OF HIS CAR

I GOT A TEMP GIG SHIPPING SOFTWARE

TWICE THE MONEY FOR SITTING ON MY ASS

Comic by Damian Carr

The Naming of Ghost Bitch (Excerpt)
John Mancuso

Randy catches his breath at the point where the deserted factories end and the well-lit city blocks take over. Right there, at the axis of blight and rebirth, stands the newest icon in Providence, The New City Steakhouse. Poised on the corner, he stares at the dazzling jewel and watches the fur-wrapped women and cashmere top-coated men proceed through a gold canopy into the restaurant. In the grass beside the valet stand, a large sign reads, "Thank You Providence For A Great Year of Serving You." Randy smells the waves of grilled onions and garlic; he fantasizes about the warmth of dimly lit oak dining rooms and steaming soups filled with big chunks of potatoes.

While watching darkened office buildings pass by the cab window, Randy reflects back to the grandness of New City. As the taxi curves around Kennedy Plaza, he looks at the bundled mass of people boarding the bus he would have taken and mumbles, "Dreaded public transportation, something transies should never deign to take." This mantra always started off the monologues of one of his oldest friends, and first idol, Goldy Digger, a recently killed drag performer who told mythological tales of fabricated extravagances. Watching the bus take off without him seems to Randy like a perfect tribute to Goldy. Whether truth or fiction, Goldy cemented his fame with a story he told at one of his legendary stand-up performances. Late in the afternoon on a Sunday in Washington, DC, Goldy told the audience, "I've been to Fire Island three times...." Then he paused in front of the indifferent crowd, took a drag from his Kool 120, exhaled and said, "Today." Another deep drag and exhale. "Once for brunch. Once to get a lipstick I forgot. And once, just because I could."

Goldy fashioned a persona out of claiming to take limos everywhere he went, though, ironically, he got killed by one. The limo's passenger testified that Goldy--

riding his real and only method of transportation, a 1979 Schwinn Co-Ed -- fell in front of the limo first. And when a coroner discovered drugs and alcohol saturating the drag queen's corpse, all charges were dropped against the driver.

Randy recalls the headlines:A sensational question: which came first: the Man, the Woman, or the Man? The passenger in the limo that night, Christopher Widemann, known as "Christy," owns New City Steakhouse. Randy remembers that Christy was en route to the restaurant's Grand Opening party that night. And at this point, three-quarters into the journey back to where Randy will sleep tonight, he puts the two glaringly obvious coincidences together. He ponders: Goldy died exactly a year ago to the day, and tonight at New City, the rich will toast Christy with Vueve Cliquot and stuff their bodies with shrimp and cream sauce on the anniversary of her death. Disrespect, he thinks, even though Goldy did love champagne.

By the time he gets to Ronnie's condo, where he squats, Randy hopes that all of tonight's party attendees get struck with painful flashes of gout and that all of the people who handle the money for Christy rob him blind: While tipping the cabby $3, Randy glances at his newly-confident mug in the rearview mirror.

* * *

Randy wears masks to shield the light that cuts through thin drapes, and earplugs to block the noise of other squatters. Jolted awake by his own nightmare, he sits up and slowly catches his breath, trying not to rouse anybody into starting their day. The minute one wakes up, they all do: repiecing the endless din of rancid wigs and rides home from the night before. Randy succumbs to the rare quiet of the room, not ready to confront the morning well underway outside. He wishes it would stay forever inert and dark, like the insurance office in Providence he managed to break into last Christmas day, the day before he started staying at Ronnie's for good.

Most of them sleep at Ronnie's once a week, fleeing their narrow, New England villages for an opportunity to entertain the mysterious forces that impel them to dress like women. Randy, however, has been considered one of three regulars living at Ronnie's for the past few months. Ronnie is generous, nurturing and hard working at his straight job, teaching mentally retarded adults, but he has rules: Nobody can use his "shit," nor can they bring too much of their own "shit" to his condo. So, Randy pays one of the other "girls" a dollar a day to use a stained hot plate and residue-bearded juicer. All he keeps besides some ball gowns in the closet are photos of his drag performances he displays on the bottom shelf of a broken end table.

Eventually, the other transies start to rouse themselves out of the knot of blankets and sleeping bags. After Randy finally finds the strength to pull off the covers, he searches the strewn luggage for appropriate interview attire. He feels confident he will get hired at New City; he waited tables every summer at all the cluttered, nautical-themed seafood shanties on the barrier island where he grew up. But then, he worked as Randy-the-boy, and now he wants to work as Randy-the-grown-woman; therefore, he must give much to consideration to what he will wear. His drag sisters offer Randy makeup, shoes, wigs and various articles of designer clothing.

Randy settles on a lilac jumper with a white turtleneck covered in tiny red hearts, white pumps and an add-abead necklace he snatched from a trick's daughter's bedroom. Cheery and conservative, he thinks.

At mid-afternoon, a gathering excitement brews with the coffee: ash trays fill up, showers run and doughnut boxes empty. They all cheer for Randy when the cab's horn honks and he bows at the front door.

X. X. X. At her stand, the hostess, Annie, uses a pencil to fill in boxes on a seating chart. "Thank you for choosing New City Steakhouse, please hold. Thank you for choosing New City Steak, please hold. Thank you for choosing New City Steakhouse, please hold. Thank you so much for holding; how can I help you?" Randy tries to observe everything he can.

Amazed by how many reservations the restaurant gets, Randy thinks about large tips left on gold credit card receipts; he dreams of not working the streets, finally getting his own apartment, a fabulous one with a view and a fireplace and a kitchen with counters and a clean oven and stove. Minutes pass without the hostess ever looking up, but Randy feels he must be patient. Randy listens to her proper diction and examines Annie's crisp white oxford shirt, long straight black skirt, thick, tortoise shell glasses and feels validated by his correct assumptions about the class of the place. Looking up at the ceiling's detailed woodwork and stenciling, he thinks of the future.

"Ma'am? Can I help you? Ma'am?" Annie snaps Randy out of his daydreams.

Without speaking, he reaches for the stack of forms on her stand.

While he fills out his application, Randy becomes Annie's respite in the pre-dinner lull, the time before her friends--the servers and cooks--arrive. Needing to share the event with somebody, Annie calls over the older cleaning ladies, vegetable chopping kids, and the other less socially desirable preparation staff to peek at Randy through a barrier of plants. With his head down, he struggles with all that the application process demands; he concentrates on recounting his whereabouts, his addresses, his identities.

Two of the kitchen kids, Lex and Leash, stand across from Annie. Annie gasps. "Oh my God, look at him!! My friends took me to this place called Lucky Changs in New York, a restaurant where the service staff is drag queens. It was cool but so weird. I should tell him to work there because they'll never hire him here."

Lex glares at her and sings, "Changs. Changs/A place for the suburban Jersey vulture/Changs Changs the Pizzeria Uno for the marginal culture."

Leash picks up the where Lex left off. "Changs Changs/Isn't it funny to get waited on by someone in drag and then stop at the gift shop for an overpriced bag?"

Annie looks confused. "You've heard of it?"

Leash sighs. "We've never been there. It's a Gothic Shock Syndrome song. But, dude, everybody's heard of it."

Walking back to her post, Annie states with a proud face, "Whatever."

Randy carries the application form, now covered with cross outs, half-finished phrases and incomplete information, back to the hostess stand. Annie glances at it and says, "Hold on. Thank you for choosing New City Steakhouse, please hold. Okay, thank you...uh...Randy, I've got your application. We will call you when and if we need you. Thank you for holding; my name's Annie; how can I help you with a reservation?"

Randy waits through the continuous phone calls. He stands, sits, reads matchbooks and occasionally makes eye contact with Annie, who sometimes makes the "one second" gesture with her finger but most often averts her eyes.

Finally, a break in the calls. Annie says, "Yes, Randy, can I help you?"

"Yeah, you told me I would speak with a manager after I finished."

"Well, the manager on duty who does interviews is preparing for a banquet that just got dropped on us. The owner should be in..." She checks her watch. "Soon, but I don't think he will want-"

Randy feels both excited and nerve-racked: His plan might come to fruition. To him, the whole thing seems so easy. "Can I wait for the owner? You see, I really want to work here. How much you think the girls pull in a night?" The phone rings again. Not waiting for a response, Randy walks into the mauve and silver Art Nouveau lounge.

A bartender arranges glasses on the racks above him.

"Hello, I'm Randy. I'm gonna be working here soon."

"Oh...uh...good, I'm Jessie, the day bartender. What will you be doing?"

"Oh, I don't know yet. I'm meeting with the owner when he gets in. I'm thinking about waiting tables, but I want to do what'll make the most money."

"Well, daytime bartending sucks. I don't make shit."

"Well, here's something if you get me a White Russian." Randy puts a twenty in the tip carafe.

Randy slurps his drink and asks for a shot of whisky before he finishes. "I'm a little nervous, of course."

"Well, I hate to scare you, but Christy can be kind of prick. So, just be cool and realize he's gonna try to trip you up."

When Jessie goes into the back to continue his inventory responsibilities, Randy realizes he's the only one in the bar, and for a long time it remains that way. Ordering a White Russian every time Jessie reappears, Randy gets drunk.

As the evening servers file into work, Annie sends them into the bar to meet the freak who will have to face their ultimate authority: Christy. They greet Randy with forced smiles and tentative speech. The girls pretend to compliment him on his hair and make-up. The boys recoil from the assault of his alcohol-fueled warmth. Some lie, telling him the owner's an easy interview, while others tell the truth. He offers to buy each of them a drink. When they say they can't, he waves his diminishing wad of cash and shouts, "Okay, sweetheart, I'll drink for the both of us then."

At around 4:30, in full narcissistic bluster, Christy arrives. He barks commands, points at unfinished duties, and scoffs at the progress of his preparation staff. They call out to Christy with status reports on back-up buckets of cut lemons, lined bread baskets, racks of chilled glasses and trays of freshly cut stacks of lettuce, tomato and onion. When he responds with more chores, the servers give him smiles to his face and stiff middle fingers to his back.

Tonight, Christy calls a meeting of the dinner shift employees. They circle around him. Just before Christy utters his first edict, Lex, now in his street clothes, throws his apron toward the hamper; it lands right into the middle of the ring of sycophants.

Leash follows Lex. Christy glares at them. "Oh, it's clear to me that you two don't care to hear what I have to say, even though it might benefit you directly."

Lex mocks drumming. "It's out with the day and in with the night. It's you guyses turn now."

Leash starts walking away. "We already punched out."

Christy shakes his head with dismay and yells, "You are not team players." They leave the kitchen.

Leash looks at Lex. "I've gotta see what this guy looks like up close."

Lex pulls a cigarette from his pocket. "Yeah, totally. I have to say the guy has got balls to come into this place looking like that."

Leash rolls her eyes, "He didn't choose to wear that, Lex. He cannot help it. It's like the way my mother friggin' plays Linda Rondstadt when she's in a good mood. He really thinks he's a woman. You are such a meathead sometimes."

They go into the bar and approach Randy. After exchanging hellos, Lex says, "Dude, are you really gonna meet with Christy?"

"Yeah, why not. I'm here to get a job. The hostess said he would meet with me."

Lex lights a cigarette, "I'd get out now if I were you. He's a pigfucker and will only be a dick to you."

Leash grabs a lighter and lights his cigarette. "The guy cannot stop saying 'upscale.' I promise he will say it at least five times in 10 minutes. I've counted."

Randy leans back and lets out a big laugh. But then, to overcome his feeling of drunkenness, he adopts an uncharacteristic air of officiousness. "I have several years of experience in restaurants and performing in nightclubs. I'm not worried."

"Whatever, dude. You can do whatever the fuck you want." Lex starts walking away.

Leash follows him. "It's just that everybody who works here is a friggin' square and they will know you're not."

They leave the restaurant.

Leash and Lex walk out into the cold. They round the corner, pull hoods over their heads and meander into a small clump of trees. They wait for their friends while the weakening afternoon light succumbs to the night that will fall all over them.

With Lex and Leash gone, Randy senses the quiet of the bar. He ponders the meanings of what they said to him. He thinks he does not like them very much and hopes that when he gets hired, all of their shifts will differ from his. All of a sudden, Randy feels the presence of the giant mirror across from him. All afternoon, he has avoided looking into it. After a few minutes, he looks up and faces his reflection, but only for an instant. Randy feels he must face his oppressor. He looks up, but again, quickly averts his gaze. One more time. A deep breath, a sigh and the burning awareness of himself. The precarious order of things collapses and the landslide begins.

> ... he has never applied for
> a job as a woman.

Does anybody really think I'm a woman?

After all, he has never applied for a job as a woman and doesn't have any identification that states his sex as anything but male. People react. They gasp and double-take. He knows this. But he doesn't spend time with those people; he runs from them. Randy tries to think about having to spend time with these people but his mind wanders to his legion of fans: the white tank-topped, light-jeaned, uninspired lot who worship any two-bit street whore who puts on a dress or habitually uses the word "fierce," the ones who put Randy's persona at the top of the fabulous club hierarchy. And then the clients. Men. Thick-fingered, deep-voiced, barrel-chested creatures who have held Randy's tiny frame in the tousled linens of motel beds. Even if they know--or don't know--that Randy is a man, they work so impossibly hard to think otherwise. They hypnotize themselves with his caricature of femininity, until finally deluded by the trappings of their arousal. They grab the aberrant lumps on his chest born from hormone treatments and tell him how much they want to kiss them. They pinch the silicone-injected mounds in his ass and tell him how turned on they are. They listen to his tales of indiscriminate sex, the pithy quips he steals directly from Rue McClanahan's character on the Golden Girls, and laugh with raucous disbelief. They stare into his made-up face and listen to the altered biology in his voice and tell him that he's sexy.

Even after these achievements--his ability to successfully entertain gaggles of image-conscious club kids and satisfy even the most macho of paying customers-- he still yearns to be a real woman. A woman. A woman in the eyes of a mirror. A woman in a furnished house and in every other private space in life. He dreams of tending plants, filing recipes, playing tennis and watching television as a woman, a glorious woman. But he must live with the cold-hearted reality, alone, late at night, when the cars driving down the alley become scarce and the "girls" he lives with fall asleep. Then, he must strip himself of the ball gowns, the wigs, the jewelry, the make-up, and most importantly the words--the pronouns, the arsenal of put-downs and clever turns of phrase--until he stands naked and silent. It's then when he must unfasten all of the hinges and reach for the truth, grab it from its hiding place between his legs and let it hang in the balance and so prominently jeer at him. It's then when he must embrace the truth, manipulate it, dance with it, for some momentary relief. And in the sticky haze of despair, when finally drifting toward sleep, Randy imagines the one fluid cut that will end all of his confusion and hide the truth for good. It's then that he recalls images of such luxury, emblazoned in his head in small, matte-finished snapshots of Susie Jackpot from the Baubles drag circuit who after surgery moved with her military boyfriend to a far away place called Camp Lejeune, North Carolina. Susie posing next to her washing machine. Susie playing bridge with the other wives. Susie hanging a wreath on the front door of her trailer. Images of hope for the future. Photos lost in the piles of junk Randy has moved around from one living room to the next.

* * *

Once the servers disperse from the pre-meal meeting, Annie assuredly strides into the halo of importance surrounding Christy. With a self-satisfied tone, she speaks. "Ah, Christy. We need to talk." Over her head, he watches the servers' progress. She continues, "You are just not going to believe this. I mean, you probably can, being a veteran in this business, but-"

"Just get to the point, Annie." Christy looks at one of his two watches.

She laughs. "There's a drag queen waiting to see you and he, she, or it, wants a job here. And, the kicker is that it has been here for hours and has been doing shots in the bar and is now wasted!" She laughs and looks toward the bar.

"What the hell? Why isn't somebody doing something about an intoxicated customer? Why did I waste money training you assholes? You know how much the binders cost for those orientation manuals? Ten bucks a pop! All of that money and you all let some lowlife get drunk and sue my restaurant for every penny I got." He walks over to a place from which he can see into the bar without Randy noticing.

Annie loudly whispers to Christy. "Do you want me to kick the person out? I will. Just tell me what you want me to say about the interview."

Christy turns around and marches back to Annie. She flinches as he approaches. "You think I care about some fucking freak? All I care about is getting him out and off of my premises, so my customers don't think I'm running some sick sideshow here. My establishment has standards. And I will only employ people who share my vision about what is and what is not acceptable. The entire team's judgment tonight has made me question whether I can trust anybody anymore."

Christy covers his face with his hands and takes a few deep breaths. He then looks Annie in the eye and speaks with an almost cautious and fragile manner. "I want to you to escort him through the kitchen and out the back door. Do not. I repeat, do not let him anywhere near the dining room. Tell him that I will meet him outside because I'm busy, or need a cigarette. I don't care what you tell him; just get him out the back door. I gotta get out of here for a minute to cool down. I'll be back in ten. And when I return, I don't want to see anybody like that in Providence's most tony dining property. Understand me?"

Annie marches into the bar with the same self-satisfied smirk. She grabs Randy by the hand. "Why don't I lead you to our fearless leader?"

"Oh, good. He's ready?" Randy gulps down the rest of his drink. "Smell my breath. Do you think he can tell I was drinking?" Randy blows in the direction of her face. Speechless, Annie's eyes open wide. Randy blows harder, motioning with his fingers. "C'mere. Come closer." Annie doesn't move.

Annie sighs. "Put your coat on, Randy."

"Why?"

"It's cold out there." Annie crosses the distance between them to help him get into the sleeves.

"What do you mean?"

"Christy has agreed to meet with you. He wants you to go outside, in the back near the dumpsters. But don't worry, he probably just wants a cigarette." They start walking toward the kitchen. "He doesn't like to smoke in front of us. You know, fearless leaders have to appear perfect."

Annie looks over at a brigade of after-work suits heading toward the bar and pushes Randy toward the kitchen door. "Follow me. Now."

In the sanitary glare of the kitchen, they stand in line, spectators in various stages of glass polishing, silverware sorting and napkin folding, all watching Randy head for the guillotine. They pause as Randy walks the plank, staggering toward the door. When he causes a wheeled cart to career into the metal prep line counter, Randy feels the excruciating import of their stares. "I want all of you to know how excited I am to work with everyone tomorrow. Hey, I'll need it. After these bar prices, I'm broke again." He pulls out the few remaining ragged bills and cackles one of his showtime cackles. As he resumes his progression toward the back door, they start offering things like "good luck" and "give him hell" through knowing, overt laughter.

While Randy takes his last few steps, it occurs to him, for the first time in hours, the reason why he is going to meet Christy: Goldy. He remembers that the plan called for getting the job first and revenge later. He stops to question why he feels nervous. After all, the events of the day transpired in his favor more than he ever predicted. And now, he stands only a few steps from meeting his enemy. Caught up in the reverie, feeling suddenly arrogant, he opens the door and screams back to the kitchen, "I'm ready for my closeup Mr. Demille. I love you all!" Everyone erupts into hysterics, and Annie pushes Randy outside.

The door slams. A blast of cold. Randy's acknowledgement of nobody there. Momentary dread. And then, he sees it: a limo in the corner of the parking lot.

He walks over to the limo. He knocks on a window and looks deeply into the abyss of its dark tint. Nothing. No one. Bastards.

He begins to force tears and pound his fists against the metal. He says to himself, "You killed Goldy." He wants to cry louder and pound harder but quickly accepts that there are no cameras, no lights.

The cold stings the wetness on his cheeks. He pulls the few bills out and counts.

When a group of kids--led by Lex and Leash--run out from behind the trees into the parking lot, Randy shoves the money back in his pocket and screams, "Please. Don't hurt me!"

Lex doesn't acknowledge Randy's fright. "Did you just get out of that limo?"

Leash laughs. "It's just like the end of Sid and Nancy. You're like one of them, a ghost coming out of a limo!"

"Yeah, man, she's fuckin' GHOST BITCH! That tune on Bad Moon Rising!" Lex screams. All the kids loudly agree.

"What were you doing in a limo?" Leash asks.

Randy catches his breath--still confused--and feels the fear inside him abate. Immediately he's able to conjure up the sounds of Goldy's inflection. "Honey, I take limos everywhere I go. Even to dumps like this."

And Lex, Leash and the thick-jacketed, sweatshirt-hooded group of kids laugh. And Randy proceeds with a monologue, punctuating Goldy's most famous punchlines with triumphant white exhales of winter air. As he rambles on about private parties in Newport mansions and at the Kennedy compound in Hyannis, the kids just listen and laugh with a dubious awe.

When one of the girls lights a joint, they form a tight circle in which Randy wedges himself. In silence, Randy watches the cigarette travel around, from one mouth to the next until it gets to his. He takes a huge hit, inhaling the smoke and any other remnants from everybody else's lips. Feeling the calm wash over him, he watches the joint go around the circle again, making its direction back toward him. He thinks: Eventually it will be in everybody's mouth and then back in mine, again and again. Randy watches the kid next to him savor the joint in his mouth and then without hesitation hand it over to him, in the same way the kid on his right will take the cigarette, without pause, from Randy's hands into his mouth.

Lex breaks the rhythm, "Hey, Ghost Bitch, tell us another one."

Imagining Goldy watching him from above, Randy looks to up at the stars becoming visible in the sky. Then, he pauses briefly, looks at all of the kids and begins assembling the words of another long story.

Photograph by Elizabeth O'Connor

Refried Marginalization
Heidi Jones with Leah Ryan

Q: Tell me about your first restaurant job.

A: I washed dishes at La Mexican Restaurant in Collegetown (names have been changed). The town is full of rich, PC people who think they care and college students who only care about themselves and marginalized locals who are just trying to get by.

Q: And where are you from originally?

A: I'm from Houston, Texas.

Q: Were you the only black person working at the restaurant at the time?

A: Yes, it was just me. I think they hired another black person after I left.

Q: That's interesting.

A: Well, everyone was so PC that nobody would ever make an issue out of it.

Q: What was the work like?

A: It was incredibly hard work. Not only washing dishes, but running for the cooks and prepping a lot.

Q: Was it a shock to you, how hard the work was?

A: No, because I had worked at Horrible Factory and for Nasty Lamp Designer (names have been changed) But it was hard. The bosses were old hippies. They used to smoke weed in the back room and think up new margarita recipes.

Q: But you didn't wash dishes forever...

A: No, a cook left, and they trained me to be a line cook. The guy who trained me had been to chef school, so I really learned a lot.

Q: What was the hardest thing about working at that restaurant?

A: PC people tend to hire the incompetent and then they don't have the guts to fire them. I had to work with this one girl who was really bad. I came in one afternoon, and she was cleaning the fryalator, and she forgot to turn the valve off and she dumped five gallons of oil onto the floor behind the stove. That put us an hour behind schedule, and we just had to deal with it. The waitstaff doesn't want to hear your problems. For a while, also, they didn't seem to want to make me the head cook, so they hired a lot of other head cooks. One guy came in with no shirt and no shoes. He was a junkie and he'd have to go boot up in the middle of the shift and then he'd come back all fucked up.

Q: What do you think would surprise the average restaurant patron about what goes on behind the scenes?

A: I think people would be surprised to find out how few people are actually putting all the food out. I think they would also be surprised to find out who those people are. Around here, it's a lot of young locals with a lot of metal in their faces. They're working-class kids, not college kids. Sometimes they get really exploited by restaurant owners, because it's the only work they can get.

Q: What's your favorite thing about being a restaurant cook?

A: I like it when you're working with somebody on a busy Friday or Saturday night and you just know what to do and nobody has to say anything. Everything just kind of happens.

Q: What's the first thing you want to do when you get out of work on a busy night?

A: I want to sit down.

What Kind of Pie Do

I am a waitress.
Part of my job is to act as if I like you.
I don't.

He always came in at 7pm, sat at the counter, winking and exclaiming, "I'm back for those *good-looking waitresses.*"

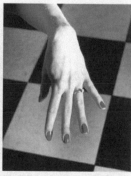

Should I wear the ring, pretend that I'm "taken," and hope they keep their comments to themselves? Or, should I take off the ring, pretend that I'm single, and hope for better tips?

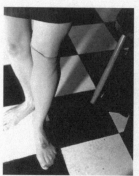

Waitresses must wear nylons because:

a.) Wholesome girls wear stockings
b.) Wearing pantyhose helps the ladies do their job better
c.) Girls' legs are less hygienic than boys'
d.) Nylons just make good, plain sense

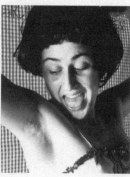

Armpit hair?

Unhappy with me because I wasn't being a good little waitress and flirting with him, he kept sending me back to the kitchen—telling me that his Bud wasn't cold enough. Every time I stuck his 'Bud' into the ice cooler, I pretended I was freezing his dick off.

You Have, Little Girl?

I greeted him in the same *my-job-is-to-be-friendly* way I greet everybody else, asking him where he would like to sit.

He said my lap would do him just fine.

I asked him if there was anything else that he needed—He suggested some table dancing.

Even the cooks agreed that his comment wasn't okay.

All of the other waitresses would whisper, "Well you *know* how Andrea makes her tips..."

He was finally leaving. Serving him had been hell. Standing at the register, he told me I shouldn't wear dresses like the one I had on. He told me I was cute. I started backing away as he tried to grab my shoulder. Finally, his wife stood in between us.

In the United States in 1988, 189,000 male waiters each earned an average of $230/week. In that same year, 432,000 female waiters each earned an average of $170/week.

If I died and went to Dante's hell, I would spend eternity as a waitress serving white men in business suits.

Ink Stain
Kate Barrett

We were a hospital family in a strange way; not in the way you would be if your father or mother was a doctor. My mother was a nurse, her mother was a receptionist in the emergency room, and her sister was a lab technician.

My mother went to the Catherine Labourne School of Nursing in Boston. It was Catholic, and run by nuns. My mother spoke of curfews, study hours and dress codes. She attended the school with a group of girls from Lowell. When she graduated, she went back to her parents' house and began to work at St. John's Hospital in Lowell, a walk past the mills over the bridge.

My brothers and sister and I went to the Immaculate Conception school, separated from the hospital by a school yard, a convent, and a road. On the first day of school each year, we made a visit to the emergency room to see my grandmother and show her our new school shoes.

When I was eight, I got a job going around to patient rooms and selling newspapers. I left a pile under the floor desk and carried as many as I could hold. I would go around and knock on the doors to see if the patients wanted to buy the paper. The Lowell Sun. My clothes got covered in ink all up the side and under the sleeve of my jersey. I had to stop on each floor and wash my hands in the bathroom because I had the habit of rubbing my face. Inevitably I stained my nose by pushing up my glasses with a finger.

The floors were laid out like a figure eight. There was a desk at the point where the eight crossed itself. I put the pile of papers under it. Nobody ever seemed to use these desks so I considered them my hiding place of safekeeping for the papers.

I couldn't carry as many papers as I could sell on one wing, so I would have to backtrack for more. This involved skulking past the open-doored rooms of patients who knew why I was there. They were on the lookout, ready to buzz the nurse if need be. They thought I was trying to get away with not selling a paper when all I was doing was trying to get them one. They would call out to me, and I hated having to stop and explain myself.

I tried to make it by with the linen carts. Sometimes a security guard would sit at the desk talking on the phone, and I would pace the floor pretending to be a visitor looking for a room number. I hung around in the handicapped bathrooms a lot, washing the ink off of my skin.

I turned the water gray. The outside paper in my stack got frayed from my hand holding it. In the fall and winter I wore long sleeves. At the beginning of the route I would carry a big stack, so big that the cuff of my shirt would get black with ink. When the clock moved and I was several floors into the route, my stack was thinner and I could hold it more with my elbow. By then my fingers were in a cramp. I was fascinated by the ink stains on my finger prints.

I was always wanting to go into the little coffee shop to get the hot chocolate that poured itself into the paper cup. But I did not want to be seen lounging around eating candy and drinking candy like a no-good bum.

My left side pocket was filled with dollar bills and quarters, my right was for pennies, nickels and dimes, and my back right was for tips. I felt like the tin man. If I forgot to bring a belt there could be a danger of my pants sliding down from the weight. The routine was, knock on the door, wait for an answer, slowly push the door open to forewarn any deaf ones, and gauge the scene.

One-patient rooms were preferable since you avoided the humiliation of several pairs of eyes on you as you struggled to hold the papers, hold up your pants, get change for a dollar, and get the dollar in the left pocket under the papers, and push up your glasses.

I had short hair, I was skinny, I looked like a boy. I was called Paper Boy, Sonny, Joe and Jack. Also Little Boy and Young Man. The friendlier types would greet me this way and continue to use these terms until they asked me what my name actually was, at which point I would mumble "Kate" as inaudibly as possible, so as to spare them they embarrassment of their mistake. My mother said I should hold my head up and loudly say "Jack!" when asked this question.

If you knocked on the door and there was no answer and you went on down the hall, it was Murphy's Law that a nurse would call after to you, berating you for breezing by the man in 302 who waited all day for the paper to come since he had no family or friends to visit him, or the woman in 420 who kept her quarter and dime ready on her nightstand but could not answer your knock since her esophagus had been removed.

My mother called me a sneaky conniver, and she was right because I spent all of my energy figuring out ways to get by these people, the dying people clutching my shirtsleeve and not letting it go as the papers slid backwards under my elbow. That was my role: symbol of youth and hope.

> My mother called me a sneaky conniver.

As the specter of death loomed on their horizon, the desperate patients waited all day until I got to their rooms with the paper so they could read the funeral notices and see everyone's name but their own.

The sight of a patient lying quietly on his back on the starched bed with the dusk settling in caused me inexplicable grief. Stepping in on them made me feel like I was spying, and most of the time I was. I wished feverishly that all the rooms had cement stoops and all I had to worry about was whether someone would open the door just as I was resting the paper between it and the screen. I craved privacy. I wanted to grant it as well.

Gloves and masks were also tricky. It seemed insulting for people to actually wear them. Plus I would never have been able to handle papers and change with rubber fingers. Ducking into one of those rooms was easier than getting out without being noticed by someone in authority. I was only caught a few times and went into a stuttering routine, holding up a newspaper as if it were a badge.

I imagined that the rooms and hallways snaking through the hospital were a giant honeycomb; tiny parts buzzing and humming to hold each other up.

There were sub-categories of the desperates: those on life support, those in Acute Geriatrics, the mentally ill and the ICU. Each terrifying to me in a unique way.

I wasn't really allowed in the ICU. The idea of walking through those doors in and among the

In ascending order I was most terrified of the ICU, Acute Geriatrics, and the Hallway Goalies.

hanging plastic, the tubes and IV poles, it almost felt like walking across the altar. One time I read the first reading at mass and I had to walk over the red carpet and genuflect halfway over when I passed the tabernacle. The atmosphere in ICU was similar in that all conversations were conducted in hushed tones and it seemed like all the shoes that walked there had extra-thick soles.

But people waiting there outside were there for days, subsisting on vending machine snacks and small paper cups of coffee. There were piles of magazines. I would drop off a couple of copies of the paper. I couldn't look at anyone. They were usually dazed and catatonic, or dazed and weeping silently, tears rolling down into the corners of their mouths.

In ascending order I was most terrified of the ICU, Acute Geriatrics, and the Hallway Goalies. These were old people who were strapped into their wheelchairs and parked right outside their rooms so the nurses could keep an eye on them. There were several varieties. They could be extremely vacant, or they could be extremely excitable, or they could be just very sick and in pain. Sometimes a comatose one would spring to life just as I was inching by. The person would start screeching like she had just been stabbed and the nurses would look over. The worst was when they screeched specific things, like, "I'm in pain!" over and over. Often it was directed right at me, and I felt really bad. I thought I should offer them the paper, but it didn't seem like they would want it or be able to read it. Thus, I felt like I was assuming they were mentally ill. Some of them seemed to be, like the ones who would say religious things like, "God the Father Almighty have mercy on me in my time of need." But, you never knew. Maybe it was a priest.

Geriatrics had dense swinging doors. No one had a room to themselves here. It felt like a prison, with up to 10 beds in one large room.

I would hear faint calls echoing desperation from the corners of the room. How could I tell who wanted the paper? I wished I could be invisible. It reminded me of standing on the school bus and being shoved into the laps of eighth-grade basketball players. The girls would aim you right at the boy they liked and shove you at him, yelling, "She wants to kiss you!" One time somebody opened the emergency door at the back of the bus, and I lurched toward it, longing to hit the pavement, but I got pulled back in before I fell.

Often I found myself giving the paper away. I had to give it free to priests and nuns, and also any relatives or neighbors I ran into. But I also left it when people were asleep, if they were regulars, and I gave it to those with no spare change.

On Sunday mornings I had to get down to the Sun building to pay the bill. There was a side door along the canal and the big green trucks with no doors would roll by. My cousin Frankie was rumored to have broken his leg taking a corner in a Lowell Sun truck.

Inside the huge building I would run under the deafening presses and up the ladder to the room hanging in the corner. I'd fork over my carefully rolled quarters, nickels, dimes and pennies and any bills I had. Then I could walk with whatever was left over.

Sundays were horrible. The papers were so thick I could only carry about five at a time. The route took a lot longer, and I got more tired and mad. Inevitably I would be covered in ink. It was harder to make change. On Sundays I had to go to the seven o'clock mass before I did my route. Once in a while I would go to mass in the chapel of the hospital; it didn't seem like mass with all the nurses and doctors and patients.

The hospital administrative offices were also on the route. These included the director of volunteers and her husband, the vice president of the hospital. The president was a nun. Some of the offices were in another building, so I had to get the key to the door so I wouldn't be locked out and have to go all the way around the front of the hospital to get back in. Getting the key meant joking with the man who kept it in his desk. Every day the same routine.

One time a man jumped out of the window in geriatrics and my mother and Esther Riopelle saw him fly by the recovery room window and heard the body smack into the gravel. Esther Riopelle was too fat to get her head through so my mother, being very slender, climbed through the window to get to the man who had jumped while Esther picked up the house phone to call the code. The nurse on the fifth floor had just left the room when the man got himself up on the window ledge and jumped with his johnny flapping behind him.

The new wing of the hospital had much larger modern windows that could only be cranked open partially, like the backseat windows in our station wagon.

There were pay phones in the lobby and three house phones. One time I was using the pay phone and I was leaning back and swinging around with the cord. A doctor who was using one of the house phones took the phone away from his mouth for a minute and said to me, "If you keep doing that, you're going to pull it out." He went back to talking on the phone and I skulked away. I was very startled because it always seemed like the doctors only talked to each other. They all sat together in the cafeteria. I don't think a doctor once even asked me to read a headline.

Waiting for the bus sitting on the bridge I would read my book, and more than a few times the bus barreled right by me, so focused I was on my reading. Then I would have to walk home, swinging change.

Illustration by Laura Kogonis

Somebody Has To Do It -- Always Immigrants
Anonymous with Moira Gentry

Q. Where are you from?

A. Dibra, Albania.

Q. How old are you?

A. 36.

Q. What is your job?

A. Cleaning.

Q. Do you work for a company or for a building?

A. I work for a company.

Q. For how long?

A. Three years.

Q. What is the worst thing about your job?

A. The truth is I don't like this job. My real profession is dental technician. I don't like the job, but I have to pay bills. The worst is... I hate to clean the bathrooms. I hate it.

Q. What is the best thing about your job?

A. Nothing.

Q. What was your worst day at work?

A. Oh... Mondays are the worst. Very bad. After two days relax, you have to start to work.

Q. What's your best day at work?

A. Thursdays and Fridays. Thursdays because you take your check, and Fridays because it is the last day!

Q. If you could tell the world anything at all about your job, what would you say?

A. If I tell from my heart, I would tell people, don't do this job but go to school, and to study. But somebody has to do this job—only, always immigrants, not American Americans. For me, who comes from Albania, I tell everybody who comes from Albania, is better to sacrifice first to go to school – try to learn for something better in your life.

Left Over
Rich Ristow

As I cleared coffee cups and plates off the table, I tried to not think about the hunger churning my stomach. Instead, I focused on my duties -- wiping down tables, stocking the salad bar, and any other stupid tasks my boss wanted. The more I thought, however, the more my empty belly ached, and when I lugged the bus tub into the kitchen, the smell of broiled steaks, creamed potatoes, and grilled chicken sharpened my torment. If I were to survive the evening, I thought, I needed to keep food out of my imagination, so I tried working harder. By focusing on cleaning tables, I tried to ignore costumers feasting around me – of all things, I feared I might do something irrational like scream at a patron, punch a waitress, or something worse.

"Harry!"

I jumped. "What the hell do you want, Nigel?"

"Stop working and look at me."

I turned from the stainless steel counter, glaring. My boss's slacks had a pronounced crease from careful ironing, and a diamond gleamed from a gold tie clip. Gossiping about his comb-over was strictly taboo. I looked at his hands, his manicured fingernails, and I thought about the people I've worked for. I sighed, fighting the urge to sneer. Out of all the restaurant managers I've met, all have groomed themselves like Wall Street day traders– everything except a sports jacket. Nigel ran for county commissioner once but was defeated during the Republican primary because he wanted to scrap health code ordinances. In a rare sense of solidarity, everybody at The Laughing Steer, from busboy to bartender, registered as Republicans, showed up at the polls and voted against him. We quickly returned to hating each other soon after.

I grimaced. "What do you want?" Without thinking, I put my hand over my stomach.

"You okay?" Nigel said. "You look very pale."

"I'm fine."

"Liar." Nigel took a piece of paper out of breast pocket, perused it, and then promptly folded it, stuffing it back where he found it. "Look. I've been organizing the schedule for next week. Can you do Mother's Day?"

"Hell no." Not that I had big plans to take my mom to the movies, but Mother's Day was a shift nobody wanted. Reservations were made year round. People, I like to think, see a free meal as an easy gift for a mother -- no pain involved, no worrying, "Will she like the book I bought?" Other "special" calendar days were not marketable because, on the Fourth of July, most people grilled out. Thanksgiving? Home cooking. It was the same with Christmas and Easter. On Mother's Day, The Laughing Steer pulled triple profits, but for some reason, all the equipment would break. Somehow, a coffee cup would get into the garbage disposal, and ceramic chunks would clog the plumbing. Last year, due to a dead dish tank, the restaurant faced 200 patrons without plates and forks. And now, Nigel wanted me to work on the worst day of the year? "Under no circumstance," I said.

"But Harry," he said. "I need you. The Laughing Steer needs you." He stared at the floor.

"I'm just a busboy."

Nobody busses tables like you.

"Nobody busses tables like you. This evening, I watched you clear a nine-seater in fifty-five seconds."

If I were that important, I thought, he'd pay me more or put me on a tip-share system. That's why I didn't like working on Mother's Day or Father's Day. The waitstaff, at least, keeps the cash left on the tables. If Nigel truly cared about me, I'd get a cut from the gratuity pool. Every time I saw more money, the federal government had hiked up minimum wage. Another hunger pang stabbed me, and I scowled.

"Harry, you sure you're okay?" He put his hand on my shoulder.

"The only problem," I said, "is the longer we talk, the more empty tables pile up. I've work to do." I turned and finished taking dirty glasses and knives out of the bus tub.

"Consider it," Nigel said. "I could make it worth your while."

"Like what?" I said. "You remember the last time I pulled a double? You gave me Laughing Steer coupons." I thought of a recent bank statement, and the balance haunted me: 52 cents. "Why do I need ten percent off, when I can't even afford to eat here?"

Shaking his head, Nigel walked away. I sighed, clutching my stomach. Jinny, a bleach blonde waitress, burst through the kitchen doors, making a line straight toward me. Before I could say anything, she started yelling.

"You lazy shit." She pointed her finger in my face. "While you've been taking your time, nobody's been seated. Why? Because you haven't . . ."

"Shut the fuck up." Before she could respond, I snatched the empty bus tub and exited.

It took me 15 minutes to clear and clean empty tables. The whole time, the agony of starving gnawed my insides. Ever since Susan, my live-in girlfriend, dumped me, I've haven't had somebody to split the cost of living with, and finding a new roommate hasn't been easy. Throughout my network of friends, nobody needed lodging space, so I resorted to classified ads in the papers. I hadn't eaten anything in a day in a half, and I had back rent to pay-- the landlady threatened eviction. To make matters worse, two months had passed since I had last sent a check to the electric company, and the utility wanted to cut me off. As soon as I got paid, I took care of the bills, which left me with no cash. My truck, facing the yearly West Virginia state inspection, needed new tires, filters, belts, and brake pads, which put my Discover Card past its limit. I had no way of buying groceries, and a death by stabbing seemed more enticing than groveling in front of my parents for money. Too many lectures came with it. My brother often complained I was too headstrong, too unwilling to let others help. I didn't believe him, and I wasn't about to ask him for cash either. He was as broke as I, but at least he worked in a restaurant that provided free meals -- Nigel thought that'd mean bad business for the Laughing Steer. "What you eat," he said often, "I can't sell, and I have a daughter to put through college." I had the next day off, and I'd decided to donate at the plasma center. Afterwards, I'd use the fifteen bucks at the supermarket, and I'd buy as much ramen noodles and canned tuna as possible. Until then, I'd drink gallons of water and dream of the future. I'd be out of college; West Virginia University would be a memory, I'd teach somewhere, and I'd write scholarly essays about M.F.K. Fisher.

After picking up after customers, I walked over to the salad bar and saw my reflection in the bottom of the lettuce bowl. I reached into my apron for a pad and pen. Then, I scribbled: pickles, croutons, green pepper, onions, cheddar cheese, pepperoni, and more. Stuffing the list into my pocket, hunger knifed me in

> Screw the customers...

the gut, and I stared at the salad bar, at the bowls of bamboo shoots and chickpeas. Two minutes, and I could eat all of it. Screw the customers – I was starting to get sick of hunger's vertigo. Shaking my head, I forced the thought away and I walked into the kitchen.

Past the grill, past ovens filled with baked potatoes and Italian bread, I ignored fry cooks dumping cheese sticks into baskets. Straight to the walk-in refrigerator I went, snatching a rolling cart.

Inside, I looked at all the shelves, at the jars of cottage cheese, the Tupperware filled with antipasto, and the portabello mushrooms marinating in marsala wine. All of it loomed, and I didn't like the temptation. A twitching, drooling starvation overwhelmed me, and I was surrounded by enough food to feed 200 people. Certainly, nobody would miss a piece of cauliflower? The Laughing Steer's profits wouldn't plummet from two missing slices of provolone? I shook my head. What if I got caught? There was a difference between on-the-job-hunger and shopping for groceries with severance pay. Times might be tough, but I'd prefer to avoid any more desperate readings of the classifieds; after all, I was already trying to find a new roommate. The more I thought about it, however, the more I couldn't shake the urge. Nigel didn't grant his employees shift meals -- we didn't even get discounts beyond the occasional coupon, and he never provided advances on paychecks. A few weeks ago, he fired a dishwasher for "stealing" steaks slated for disposal. What was I to do? I'd already gone a day and half without eating, and I couldn't last much longer. I didn't want to eat the salad bar supplies, but I thought about Nigel's manicured fingernails and didn't care.

I snatched a stalk of celery and munched it quickly. I felt a little bit better, and the celery tasted juicy, good. Without thinking, I snatched another stalk and shoved it into my face. Chewing, I glared around the walk-in fridge, wondering. What next? It wasn't a debate any more. Clenching a fistful of bacon bits, I tilted my head back and gobbled it like candy. My stomach started feeling better, but not good enough -- the potato salad beckoned. I reached over, swiped the crock pot, and ripped the lid off. Using two fingers, I shoveled chunks of potato, garlic, and hard-boiled egg into my mouth, gasping between swallows. Watery mayonnaise ran from my mouth and over my cheeks and chin. Behind me, the door to the walk-in fridge opened.

I turned.

Nigel stood in the doorway, holding a clipboard.

I dropped the empty potato salad container, hearing it clatter against the tile floor. Instinct made me wipe my face on my sleeve.

Nigel frowned, and he turned away, slamming the door.

For two minutes, I thought about how to act, but I didn't know what to do. What could I do? I stuck with my initial impulse: Act like it didn't happen. Reaching into my pocket, I retrieved the list detailing the salad bar's needs, and after I assembled all the items on the cart, I wheeled the provisions out. Then I searched The Laughing Steer for something to do. Five tables needed clearing, and after that, nothing else.

Closing time crept up, and when all the customers left, I dissembled the salad bar and put all the leftovers back into the walk-in fridge. By this time, I did my job, no longer famished. Afterwards? I helped the dishwashers scrub out cheese-crusted pots, and I rolled silverware into napkins while tuning out gossiping waitresses. Nigel lurked neaby, but I ignored him by volunteering to mop the kitchen floor. I thought about losing my job, which made me scrub that floor until it shone the reflection of lightbulbs. Toward the end of the evening, I looked for things to do, but found myself standing at a waitress station. Jinny came from behind, tapping me on the shoulder. I cringed.

"Nigel wants to talk to you."

I didn't respond -- I just walked to the manager's office, wondering how I to explain myself. When I knocked on the open door, Nigel had his nose stuffed into spreadsheets and ledgers. Waving, he motioned me to sit on a nearby steel chair.

I stood.

After three minutes, he turned and yawned, digging into his breast pocket. He pulled out a crumpled piece of paper and grinned.

"Harry, I've scheduled you for an evening shift on Mother's Day. And I also may need you for lunch." He sighed. "What do you think about that?" Before I could answer, he started laughing. "You look so much healthier. You clocked with a pale face, and now," he reached up and patted me on the cheek, "you got some color back."

"I'll do it, sir."

"You'll do what?"

"I'll work Mother's Day." No way would I bring up the earlier incident, and if Nigel was letting me off that easy, I couldn't argue.

"That's all. Get out of my office."

I walked into the kitchen. The fry cooks had left for the evening, and the chefs had begun placing frozen loaves into the ovens. Slow cooking ensured fresh bread in the morning. Trash hadn't been taken out, so I dragged all the cans to the rear exit. For a moment, I thought about getting caught wrist deep in the potato salad. I remembered the sick, painful feeling of hunger; working extra shifts wasn't the worst punishment. Nigel could've fired me. I looked into the garbage, seeing biscuits, onion rings, and baked potatoes wrapped in foil -- leftovers I wasn't allowed to take home. I tied knots in all the bags, and one by one, I hauled them to the dumpster.

Photograph by Elizabeth O'Connor

Illustration by Laura Kogonis

Jessamyn Smyth
Dancer

"Come on, baby, you could come down here, I can get you an apartment, you wouldn't even have to work…I could take care of you."

She doesn't answer, just smiles and keeps dancing, her thinly veiled crotch at eye-level. He looks up at her face, though, her pretty face above him on the platform.

"I'm serious, you know. You don't think I'm serious." He turns away and stomps over to the bar.

He's sure there's something real between them now. They talk to each other every time she works. He doesn't feel right anymore paying for her time. He glances over; she's taking a five in the g-string. He scowls at the customer. Comes back to the edge of the stage, leans on it, pulls his elbows back when they stick to the grime.

"Come out with me. Have breakfast with me when you get off." She shakes her head. He's been asking for weeks, playfully at first, more and more seriously. She just waves him off every time, like he's nothing. Smiles at him. Like she's too good for him or something, like she's not a fucking stripper.

"Why the hell not? What's wrong with me?" He jabs the air with his beer bottle. He realizes his voice is carrying across the room and the bartender is eyeing him. He tries to unknot his stomach, lowers his voice and his beer. "Come on. It's only breakfast."

"You know I can't do that," she says, offering the gentling smile. She speaks with just enough volume to make sure only he can hear her over the music, keeps her face turned away from the other customers, barely moves her lips. "You know I'd get hurt if I said yes to people who asked me out here." His face beneath her is outraged. She jumps in before he can respond, using the little-sister voice: "Come on, you know it's true, I have to say no. All I do is dance. If I said yes to you, other people would expect me to say yes to them. You're a nice guy. I know you're different, I'd be safe with you, but you know I can't say yes."

He lowers the beer bottle, feels himself loosen. She doesn't mean to be snotty, she's just scared, he thinks. She is very near, looking down at his face. She looks kind to him. Genuine. There's something different about her, different from the others. She's under his skin.

"I know you just dance. That's why I like you, want you to go out with me. Just breakfast, you know?" She doesn't answer, just shakes her head a little as she moves. "I promise I won't even touch you. I'll open the door for you." She smiles at this. He's encouraged. "I'll talk to you, listen to you. I'm a good listener. Really, give me a chance. I won't touch you. I just want to take you out. I won't even kiss you."

She is nearing the end of her set. She knows her smile looks tired as she keeps shaking her head no. A customer at the other end of the stage lays a twenty on the lip of the platform, calls her over to him. She has to get moving, this regular is eating her tips. She has to get her set-drinks lined up, too.

"Let me go," she says to the regular. "Buy me a soda after my set and we'll talk, okay?" He nods, grudgingly.

She turns and crosses the stage slowly; eyes locked on

the waiting customer, working the twenty. She gives him his illusion, his purchased seduction. Makes a living. She can't afford to piss either one of these guys off. Dance on that line, she thinks. Careful. Think tuition.

Her regular follows her part of the way, a couple of steps behind. She keeps an eye on him in the mirror. "GOD, what an ass!" he shouts. "I'd like to…" He makes a spanking motion with his hand. She closes her eyes for a moment, willing him to go away. "What I could do with you over my knee!" The bouncer approaches. The guy raises his hands, shrugs, stalks back to the bar. She likes this bouncer, the big biker. He pays close attention, protects her, keeps guys like this—tip-blockers—out of the way so she can do her job.

The twenty rests on the stage-edge. It buys a flash. The customer has a speck of spit at the corner of his mouth, and he stares at her pussy with the familiar vacant but hungry stare, as if heavily medicated. Pussy and Thorazine cause the same expression, she thinks. Why is that?

The song is winding up. He crooks his finger at her. "Bring it closer," he commands, holding up the twenty. "Turn around." Yeah, I figured you for a bend-over guy, she thinks.

Last thing you want | Yeah, 1 figured you for a bend-over guy. | is a face. Whatever.

She does the deed, bending and spreading her legs enough so he gets the view he wants. He runs the twenty across her crotch.

"Let me see it again," he says, poking her with the cash. Bastard, she thinks. She smiles seductively and reaches between her legs, teasing aside fabric with her darkly painted nails. The way they want it. Wipe your mouth, you freak. And just give me the fucking money. You think I'm up here for my health?

"You want to put it in my thong?" She asks, blinking rapidly at him upside-down through her legs. She uses the stage-voice: six year-old meets porn queen. It works on all of them. "You're not supposed to touch me, but the bouncer can't see where you're sitting... It'll be our secret."

She knows the bouncer is watching very closely, or she wouldn't offer. This guy has the tense vibe. Everyone has noticed him. The customer knows he's being watched, too. He looks around for the bouncer, sees that he's all the way across the pit at the bar. He estimates the giant's speed, decides he's got time. Instead of putting the twenty under the hip-lace of her thong where everybody lets guys put money, he stuffs his hand directly under the thong and into her crotch, forcing his knuckles hard against her labia. She jerks away.

"Fucker," she says, under her breath. The guy is smirking. The bouncer materializes and asks if there's a problem, sticking his stomach out and gripping the edges of his leather vest. He towers over the customer while he looks up at her and raises his eyebrows.

How bad? His face asks.

She shrugs. Not too.

"I'm done anyway," she says, reaching down the front of her underwear and yanking the cash out. She walks into the dressing room with a straight spine. She hears the bouncer rumble to the scumbag: "You might find the air more comfortable outside."

"Fucker," she says again, closing the curtain to the dressing room so she can wash her armpits and count her tips before going back out to the bar. It's her sixth set, out of eight—almost done. Her leg muscles twitch for a few minutes when she sits down. Exhausted. Wired. She washes the sweat from under her arms, kicks off her high heels and dumps powder into them. Washes her crotch, too. Who knows where that twenty has been. She lays a towel over the dirt and streaks of mascara before she sits on the counter and soaks her feet in the sink, counting bills. Sixty for the night, plus 240 so far. I'll do about 400. A little less. Not too bad for a Thursday. She knows the regular is waiting for her back at the bar. Her admirer. What is he again? House-painter? She stalls for a few minutes so she doesn't have to spend a full half-

hour talking to him. Plans. She has to get him to buy her a minimum of two drinks, and keep him appeased enough that she doesn't end up finding him waiting for her on the road out of town at the end of the night. Fifteen minutes of talk before she can reasonably leave him to ready for her next set. He's a nice enough guy, as far as they go here. No big deal. You can do almost anything for fifteen minutes.

He waits for her at the bar. When she comes out, she's wearing a floral silk camisole and jeans. Almost homey, not slutty at all, he thinks. She looks good. He watches her cross the room toward him. Her hips roll, breasts sway, her eyes are on him. Like I'm the only guy in the room. His chest swells with pride. She's mine, he thinks. I'll have her.

They are sitting side by side on the tall bar-stools. He presses his thigh against hers. She ignores it. She can see he didn't expect there to be awkward silences and knows she should supply some bright chatter, but she doesn't feel like it. The music thumps.

"So what do you like to do when you're not here?" he asks finally.

"I read," she says, finishing her first Coke.

"Oh yeah? What do you like to read?"

"Oh, you know, everything," she says. "I'm a real book junkie."

"Book junkie, that's funny, you make me laugh, you know that? You're funny." He is gazing at her as if it has just occurred to him that she exists. She blinks at him.

He's not a bad guy, she thinks. Not tipping me, either, though, is he. Still, it's a set-drink. This job dehydrates like crazy. Her mind wanders as he rambles. What's with the book questions? She thinks about the quiet guy who put forty bucks on the stage at her feet and asked her to just talk to him, to tell him what her favorite books were. She told him, dancing all the while, and he handed her the money. "Thank you very much," he said. He never even looked at her body. Weird. They want to be in my head, too.

"You want another soda?" He asks.

"Yes, please." She says. She watches the bartender put a twelfth check mark next to her name in the ledger next to his sink. Two for each break.

"What are you thinking about?" Says the regular.

"Oh, nothing much." She can't wait to go home. Maybe Fi will draw me a bath and rub my feet. She has such strong hands. We need to go grocery shopping tomorrow.

"You know what, I should get ready for my next set. You're really a sweet guy. Thanks for the soda." She stands. He reaches for her, puts his hand on her waist. She stiffens, gives him The Look. Don't go there, pal.

"Hey, it's all right," he says. "I just want to say thanks for talking with me."

"You're welcome," she says, a little crisply. His hand wanders upward. His eyes look teary.

Oh Christ, he's gone maudlin now, she thinks. Like I need this.

"Could I just… touch your…" His hand rubs her breast through the camisole. "You are so beautiful," he says, "I'm telling you, I could take good care of you…"

She takes his hand in hers and places it down on his thigh. Keeps her touch gentle. Doesn't show distaste, exhaustion. Looks into his eyes. Says, in a carefully firm but friendly tone: "No. Thank you, but no." She turns away and heads for the dressing room. Second to last set. As she's moving away, she hears someone at the bar say:

"What's with you and that girl, anyway? She ain't all that much."

"I don't know man," he says. "There's just something about her… Something about her really gets to me." His voice trails after her as she goes behind the curtain. "She just isn't like the rest."

Oh, yes I am, she thinks as she takes off her clothes again. You have no idea.

Dr. Clam Sauce
David Gershan with Leah Ryan

Q: Tell me about your first restaurant job.

A: I was fucking like 14. My father got me a job at a Jewish deli. Of course he didn't like ask me if I wanted a job. He just arranged the whole thing and said "Go, you have a job." So there I was standing there with all these sweaty Jewish guys. I used to have to run the register when the wives had a migraine. They called it "making change." They'd say, "David, go make change."

Q: Sounds pretty dismal.

A: And of course they didn't let you eat anything. So I would run into the cooler and I would just cram stuff into my mouth. I would just pack it in there and I like couldn't breathe. Then they'd call me, "David, go make change," and I'd be all apoplectic with a pickle shoved in my mouth. That job was my introduction to restaurant sneakers. They're horrible and can only be worn at work. If you don't leave them at work, what do you do with them? You can't bring them anywhere.

Q: What about your next job?

A: My father managed a place called the Charcoal House. I was the busboy and I used to get stoned with the grill guys. They all wore dark sunglasses in the kitchen and I used to wonder, how do they know when the steaks are done? Then I found out that my father was fucking half the waitresses.

Q: And then?

A: In the 1970s I lived in Ithaca New York and I worked at a place called Johnny's Big Red. It was a college hangout. It was ancient. When the glaciers moved at the end of the Ice Age they created the finger lakes and Johnny's Big Red. They wouldn't feed us and we were always starving. The chef was a real misanthrope. One time I was just taking a big whiff of some food because I was starving and he was standing there watching me. The best thing that happened to me when I was working there was that I was on my way to work and I was late and it was in the middle of one of those horrible Ithaca winters with ice and slush and I had to walk up all these hills. I was hitchhiking frantically. This carload of frat boys went by and hit a puddle and slushed me on purpose. I tried to make them crash, like what's that girl's name? Stephen King...?

Q: Carrie.

A: Right. Carrie. Three blocks away from where they slushed me, they swerved and hit another car. I had a good night at work that night. Then I decided I wanted to study woodworking and I moved to Rochester.

Q: Another restaurant...?

A: Cafe Left Bank. The owner, Alain, was Algerian. Brilliant. I learned a lot from him. I waited tables and I also cooked. We were so busy we didn't have time to hire more help. I worked every day. I didn't even have time to spend my tips. Then this guy started coming in, a VP from Xerox or something. We used to chat about movies, then we went out to a movie. Then we started making out. I became his lover. He even took me on a trip to New York. Turns out he was married and had three kids. That was it for me. Then I moved to Berkeley.

Q: You worked in a hippie restaurant, I bet.

A: Awful. On Telegraph Avenue. Nobody came in. We had to cook like two omelets a day. The manager was a mean dyke with no imagination. She was just learning how to hate men and she used me as a target. She fired me because I refused to throw a genius bossanova guitar player out of the restaurant. The next day I knocked at the back door of Chez Panisse.

Q: Wow, what happened there?

A: They had me come in and mince a shallot for them. That was my interview. Thanks to Alain, I started cooking at Chez Panisse full time. The food was genius.

And then I decided to go to med school. I was pre-med; I ended up on the night shift at Dunkin Donuts in the Castro.

Q: What was that like?

A: It was amazing. All these fucked-up young people would hang out. You know when you're in your 20s and you meet a bunch of people and you don't know them at all but you feel like you've known them forever? Dunkin Donuts was like a culture unto itself, a sub-freak culture. All I did was wipe the tables with a rag that I don't think anybody ever washed. After Dunkin Donuts closed, they would all go to the cafe across the street and sometimes I would follow them over there. They were just so beautiful to watch.

Q: And now you're a doctor.

A: But I'm making clam sauce, right now. While I'm talking to you.

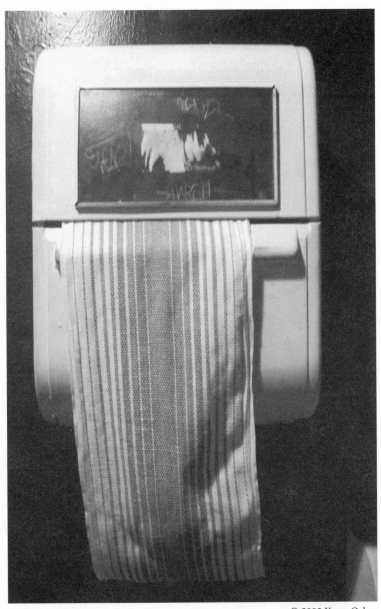

Carhop
Catherine Daly

When my parents' friends bought Elam's Silverfross Root Beer Stand, I got my job as a Carhop to keep their daughter company. The Fountains, working the soda fountain, were male. Carhops were female. We started working Sunday afternoons in April. No one else wanted this shift. Unless it was a perfect Sunday afternoon, it was slow. It only got busy a few times in May and June, after it warmed up, but before it got hot.

Onions

Until I did onions, I wondered how hamburgers at most fast food restaurants have square onion bits instead of onion loops.

Two orange clapboard cottages sat at the back of the root beer stand lot. Pepe's family rented one. His mother was a cook. The other cottage, behind the menu billboard, was used as storage and for making root beer. On a rainy Sunday afternoon, Bea and I went back to the storage cottage with Arleen, the thin, religious cook, and Debbie, the large, quiet cook and mother of Annette, the loudest and largest Carhop.

The room that had been a kitchen had a deep, stainless steel sink, a flat of 100-pound bags of white onions, and a grate. The grate was an onion-sized metal bucket with a sharp grid bottom and an attached handle that lowered to punch onions through the grid. Above the sink, a paper towel dispenser held the same hard brown towels that were in the bathrooms at school.

First you stand over the sink with knives. You cut away both ends of each onion and slice one side. You dump the peel into one side of the sink, the onions into the other side, which is filled with ice water. You do this until the peelings and onions accumulate. A strong wave of vapor comes up from the onions. You can almost see the fumes.

At this point, after about 15 minutes, Bea would have to leave. Some people are more allergic to onions than others. Your eyes and nose start to run, so you grab the towels, but that brings your onion-covered hands closer to your face. You might even get onion on your face. That's the worst thing. One trick is to just let your eyes and nose go and breathe through your mouth. The cooks didn't have to watch their hands or knives, so they turned their faces away, toward the radio, and talked to each other. I had contact lenses, so I was more immune to the fumes.

Debbie started punching the onions through the grate into a plastic bucket. Arleen fed the grate. When the plastic bucket was full of onion squares, she dumped them into a plastic bag and tied it. She and Arleen did most of the work. I skinned only one big bag of onions. Annette replaced Bea and picked up the pace. I was still slower than Annette when she moved to the puncher so Debbie could cut for us and we could all leave at the end of the day shift.

One of the Fountains picked up the bags and took them to the freezer. The cooks cleaned up. As I left, another Fountain came outside with my time sheet and my split of the tips (which we pooled when it was slow) and an extra $5 for doing onions. It was a cold and rainy Sunday and I wouldn't have made that much ordinarily. When I got home, Mom made me shower immediately.

Gum

We weren't supposed to chew gum while we worked. "You girls look like cows chewing cud," the manager would say.

There was one two-sided metal station on a concrete curb between every two parking spaces. The stations were metal, and each side held a plastic-covered menu that was lit at night, and an intercom with a button next to it. The spaces were numbered, consecutively around the lot and under the canopy. A switchboard inside lit up and buzzed when a station button was pushed. The person working the board would then switch on the speaker and take the order.

Bea and I scraped stations with razor blades. Customers throw or spit their chewing gum out the window as the food arrives. We cleaned the stations, the curbs, and the asphalt around them. This was a bad job. We did it early in the season, when it was cold, when the lot was empty and the gum was hard. We started at station one. Stations one through six were never bad because they were next to the stand. People were less likely to spit gum where we might see them.

The gum blobs were gray, but after we sliced and scraped them, we could see which flavor they had been, the color. Sometimes we could smell it. We guessed what kind of gum a glob would be. Bubble Yum was the worst -- large, sticky blobs that stayed soft and sticky no matter how cold it was. We chewed that brand. It was important not to think about the mouths that had chewed the gum.

Old Cars

There is no law that says vintage cars have to visit drive-ins, but this is what happens. I was lucky, since before I got my driver's license, I was car crazy. I deliberately "tried" for orders that were from vintage cars I wanted to see. Their drivers were usually cheap, as if they thought root beers were still five cents as they were when their car was new, or they did the stand a favor by coming, and their food should be free.

Big Tipper

The Carhops took turns for Roy, who had a big burgundy truck. He was older than most customers, and had a big ZZ Top-style beard. I'm sure Roy was not a ZZ Top fan. He ate the same order every lunch: salad, large iced tea with Sweet 'N' Low, and a deep-fried pork tenderloin basket with extra tomato, lettuce, and mayonnaise. Baskets were a sandwich, fries, and a shot-sized cup of coleslaw served in a red or yellow plastic basket lined with white waxed paper stamped with a 50's style black and orange line drawing of the stand. Roy left the change from the amount and two dollars.

After three or four turns, which might take a whole season, he'd talk to you a little. But even after five years, I wouldn't say we ever had a conversation. There were Carhops who had been there 10 years or more, and he talked easily with them.

Strange Tippers and Rain

We did not wear roller skates.

Carhops wrote names on slices of white pickle containers with a big black marker (if we had time, we decorated them as well) and put one on each tray we brought out. That way, we knew whose tips were whose, and, since no one liked taking trays in, who should really pick up the trays.

We wore white shirts with a collar and black pants or shorts. Fountains were encouraged to wear black bow ties.

When it rained, guys would park at the farthest stations and order one item at a time. One root beer. Then they would know their Carhop's name. When they placed another root beer order, they'd ask for her. Then fries. Onion rings. A shake. A cheeseburger. Another cheeseburger. The goal was to get the Carhop's shirt wet. We did get big, wet tips that way, usually all the change from all the orders.

Sometimes guys wrote love notes on napkins. Once, a guy left me a handful of unidentified pills.

Male Carhop

There was one male Carhop. He was short and had blond curly hair. He had carloads of "girlfriends" come by and leave him big tips. While he usually made more tips than we did, some customers would complain.

Inside Regulars

The stand was at the west end of the popular cruising street. Eldorado (long a) was a straight, four-lane street that divided town from highway to highway, but it still had sidewalks. It had Long John Silver's and two McDonald's, Dairy Queen, Hardees, Wendy's and Rax, and another drive in, called Taylor's, at the east end. The root beer stand was between a railroad overpass and the Mueller Castings employee parking lot.

The customers who ate at the counter inside were different. Elderly people came in for breakfast. Odd people wandered in off the street, especially after Adolph Meyers, the local mental health hospital, closed. A few roving Vietnam vets had to eat outside. A quiet lady with puffy brown hair, always neatly dressed in white blouse and dark suit, called ahead with her order, then came in a cab. Usually the cab waited for her. She never spoke after she was seated at the counter. She used a whole dispenser of paper napkins and then took another pile home.

Abe came to the high school football games as well as to Elam's. He would stand on the sidelines by himself and cheer through a waxed paper Pepsi cup with the bottom punched out, like a little red-white-and-blue megaphone. He wore a stovepipe hat and black greatcoat and talked about Illinois history. Once he paid for his coffee with a Civil War-era silver dollar, thinking is was still worth only a dollar. When Abe wouldn't take it back, he got a credit for its worth. Right before Abe died, he came in wearing a different outfit. He'd bought a velvet wall hanging of the Last Supper from a gas station down Eldorado, cut armholes in it and wore it as a vest. He offered people silver dollars if they could name the apostles.

Drive-Throughs

If just-married couples drove through the lot on the way from the church or reception, they got a free quart. No one ever dressed up and pretended to be just married for the free quart. Not only cruiser weddings did this – just anybody getting married in town.

Because Elam's wasn't a chain, but was on the main drag, people doing things like riding funny three-wheeled bikes cross country would stop at Elam's. Salesmen would try to distribute odd stuff, like cardboard comb cards or aspirins in little metal boxes.

Employee Food

You tend to eat strange things, or strange combinations of things, from the menu of the restaurant where you work. I ate deep fried pork tenderloin patties without the buns as a kind of a cracker for lettuce, tomato, and mayo; tamales with chili on top; Coney dogs, which are chili dogs, except the chili is beanless, with cheese and onion. Only employees and Roy ate the salad. Bea turned me on to Hostess fruit pies heated in the microwave with soft serv on top, butterscotch-and-chocolate malts, and everything soda, which had a shot of all the sodas at the fountain, plus, of course, root beer.

The Food

The hot fudge sundaes were particularly good. The fudge itself was the best I've tasted. I don't know the brand. It came in #10 cans with a retro label. The soft-serv, which is ice milk pumped through a special machine, not scooped out of tubs like regular ice cream, didn't have as much air pumped in as at other fast food restaurants. It was a darker cream color. By comparison, Dairy Queen soft serv, which may use a milk product as a base, is almost all air. Sundaes were served in small blue plastic dishes.

Crystals of frozen root beer form on the ice cream in a black cow, which is the reason that a black cow is something more than just root beer and ice cream. Ice cream makes the root beer fizz too much, however, and so black cows were topped off twice, once before the black cow left the stand, and then from a small cup the car hop would carry out with the food. An orange cow, soft serv with orange flavored soda, is disgusting looking. Something about the orange pop makes small bits of soft serv float to the top, which looks like vomit. It tastes fine, if you like orange pop.

The Bigger Beef Burger (3B) was the largest hamburger, one-third of a pound at least. It seemed much larger than one-third of a pound of beef. The Elam's sign proclaimed the "world famous" deep-fried breaded pork tenderloin sandwich. The tenderloin was easily eight or nine inches long, extending inches beyond the large seeded bun, but it was very thin and crispy. Eating it was like eating a bread sandwich. The most expensive item on the menu was the shrimp basket with onion rings substituted for fries, which was $3.99 + .50 when I started.

Root Beer

Root beer is not my favorite drink. It's herbal, from sassafras. Elam's originally bought its extract from a company called Silverfross. The appeal of root beer for me lies in its frosty mugs and head of foam. Root beer is absolutely not the same in stores or with ice. Mugs were kept in a bath of very cold water, so that when they were removed from the bath, they developed a coating of frost. The perfect head was slightly over the rim and almost an inch thick. The stereotypical mug was the large, although it was difficult for most customers to drink a large. People stole the mugs constantly.

> We weren't supposed to read.

Entertainment

We waited in line for orders, separated from the Fountains by a counter. There was a narrow plywood shelf we weren't supposed to sit on underneath an old plastic Pepsi clock. There were trays on the shelf. We weren't supposed to sit at all.

We weren't supposed to read. Fountains would occasionally throw mugs of water on us. We would occasionally get into wars with ketchup packets, smashing the packets in a certain way so that the ketchup could be aimed. I usually cut a New York Times crossword puzzle out of the paper and hid it near the white plastic pickle containers we sliced up for tip cards.

I would also try to adopt a new personality or accent for each order, which, needless to say, didn't work very well.

Assembling a Tray

The orders were entered into the computer, which had a touchpad for each food item. It printed the receipt in blue and "The Customer is Always Right" and "Be Nice to Every Customer" in red. Order modifications, including specific Carhop names, extra crispy fries, and seven-up floats, were written on the receipts. The food order and any milkshakes were called out and then posted through the pass through window to the cooks.

The cooks placed most of the food items under the heat lamps as they came up:

fries and onion rings on our left, their right, near the fryer; baskets and sandwiches on our right, their left. They put salads on a separate shelf or handed them to us. When the order was completely up, the cooks put the receipt up.

We assembled orders from the receipt, putting the food on the far side of a brown plastic tray with either a red or green Handi Wipe covering it. The food was on the far side since it was lighter than the root beer in mugs. The Handi Wipes kept mugs and food from sliding on the tray. As we took the food out from under the heat lamps, we called out the drinks and desserts to the Fountains. If the drink was root beer it was named only by size.

We put the coleslaws, which were in a tub above a tub with ice in it, in baskets. If there was a basket, and hence coleslaw, we added a fork. Scooting the tray along a counter, we added two ketchups for every deep fried thing, two salts, pepper and mustard only if it was requested, and napkins on top of the food.

By the time we'd distributed the condiments, the drinks were up. The heavy glass root beer mugs were easier to carry on the close end of the tray, so they had to be lifted up and around the food, so they wouldn't drip on the food. At the end of a shift, the front of your shirt would be covered with root beer.

For quarts or gallons, we went outside to the refrigerator case and brought them in to be topped off. They were half-filled so that they wouldn't lose their fizz, but wouldn't take as long to settle as a just-poured container of root beer.

We had $20 dollar banks in two-pocket aprons like those that carpenters tie around their waists to hold nails. As we stacked a tray, we paid for the order so that we'd have correct change for the customer. Customers always avoided pennies, with, "Here are three pennies so I can have a quarter", etc., which of course you didn't have unless you could take it from your tips. If you couldn't, you had to go back in to get "silver money", which meant you lost your turn in the order pick-up line. On the way back to the stand, you were supposed to bus trays in from the stations and clean them up.

Bees

Root beer contains a lot of sugar and draws bees. The hotter the weather, the more bees there are in a root beer stand. Fountains would go onto and over the railroad siding, where there were trees, to look for hives to destroy, but bees had learned to come to the root beer stand.

At the height of bee season, no one picked up trays if they could avoid it. Even empty root beer mugs drew bees. There would be not a few, but many bees on each mug, dead bees floating, bees underneath the waxed paper wrappings if root beer had been spilled. You had to shoo the bees before bringing the trays inside.

Orange

Elam's color was orange. The stand and canopy, cottages, the color on the wrappings, the counter tents printed with the breakfast menu, rain slickers: all orange. Orange was also the wall color in my great uncle's restaurant, a former diner, farther down Eldorado, where my parents and their friends had trained in the restaurant business. Orange is said to increase appetite, or make one hungry.

Although business slowed after Labor Day, each season ended at Halloween with a party inside the stand. The candy counter was cleared out; dribs and drabs of food that would not last until April was divvied up; there was champagne. The giant rattling plate-glass windows would frost over.

Molly O'Dell's Restaurant and Bar Employee Manual Revisions
Anne Earney

Changes to the employee manual are effective immediately for ALL employees, whether or not employees have received a copy of the manual, read the manual, or were aware a manual existed.

All employees are required to read the manual in full. Management may quiz employees at any time. In the event that an employee cannot read, it is that employee's responsibility to find someone to read the employee manual out loud. If an employee is unable to do so, a note explaining the difficulty must be presented to management within 90 days of beginning employment.

Vacation

1 All vacations must be approved by management. Employees must give two weeks notice prior to the start of any vacation. Management may, at their discretion, especially in the case of female employees, accompany employees on vacation, in which case employees must forfeit vacation pay to management. All vacations with management will be taken in Las Vegas. All frequent-flier miles will accumulate on management's accounts, and all winnings, whether by management or employee, are the property of management.

2 In the event of an involuntary unforeseen absence involving prison time, management must be notified of the expected period of incarceration if employment is desired upon release. Management is not responsible for bail or bond. Employees must file written requests for care packages. Only two care-packages per employee per prison term. Requests for items in care packages not approved by prison officials

(e.g., drugs, guns, home-brewing kits) will be ignored. All prison time counts towards yearly vacation allowance. Vacation pay is not given for prison time. Additionally, management is not responsible for the legal costs incurred by the employee, and employees are encouraged to make use of a public defender like other common criminals. Management understands that the occasion legal infraction cannot be avoided, but please try to keep these to a minimum.

Employee Drinking, Smoking and Drug Use

1 No employee drinking, on or off the clock! Management must be unaware of employee drug use.

2 If a customer wants to buy an employee a drink, management approval must be obtained before employee consumes the drink. All "bonus" drinks are to be shared with the approving manager. Employee will let management drink their half first. Employee may not complain about the size of the remaining "half."

> **Please do not use Molly O'Dell's aluminum foil for marijuana pipes...**

3 If an employee is caught drinking, a receipt for the drink must be produced. Any employee drinking without a receipt will be fired for stealing! All employees caught with drugs will surrender the drugs to the on-duty manager. If the employee does not ask questions, the police will not be notified. Management will return to work after one to two hours, depending upon type of drug seized.

4 DO NOT leave paraphernalia lying around! Please do not use Molly O'Dell's aluminum foil for marijuana pipes, dart tubes for crack pipes, or plastic bottles for water bongs. Do not leave straws lying on counters in the restroom.

5 Smoking is allowed only in designated areas, restroom stalls, and that corner in the

kitchen where there is no camera. Any employee responsible for a fire on the premises will be required to perform the "rain dance" during the dinner rush on the Friday night following the fire. Specifics of rain dance will be determined by management and may include but are not limited to partial nudity, tar, and feathers.

6 Any bartender caught serving employees will be fired on the spot! Remember, it is unethical to serve known alcoholics! However, bartenders should serve paying customers as long as they have cash, credit, or jewelry. If necessary, bartenders may stop serving a customer who has vomited on, urinated on, or otherwise defaced the bar or another customer. If said customer is also an employee, bartender MUST inform management before throwing customer/employee out, as employee may still be on the clock and not allowed to leave.

7 DO NOT give cash or drugs to the kitchen staff. If any employee sees a member of the kitchen staff talking to suspected drug dealers in the alley behind the building, inform management immediately. Any kitchen employee too strung out to perform basic cooking duties or prep work will be sent home, or to wherever it is the kitchen employees stay. Dishwashers may no longer sleep in the alley between shifts due to sanitation concerns.

8 If you suspect you are drunk, and the manager on duty is too stoned to notice, you have the right to send yourself home. All work duties must be completed prior to leaving. As employees are not permitted to make outgoing calls on the bar phone, employees will need to step out onto the street to hail a cab. DO NOT get run over! We will not be responsible for bodily damage incurred in such a manner.

Theft

1 Restaurant and bar supplies are not for personal use. Employees may not "borrow" supplies for their bachelor parties, wedding celebrations, keg parties, or wakes.

2 If an employee invites a member of management to the employee's residence and management recognizes dishware, barware, customers, or sanitation supplies from Molly O'Dell's, management has the right to confiscate all drugs and alcohol on the premises.

In the Event of Illness

1 Management requires 48-hour advance approval for all paid sick leave. Employee must call management in person to report illness, injury, or death. If the employee is unable to do so, as in the case of paralysis, coma, or amnesia a medical professional may call. No employee's mother, neighbor or girlfriend is considered a "medical professional."

2 If an employee becomes ill or injured while on the clock, management will clock employee out and deny any knowledge of employee's presence on premises. Remember, a perfect record with workmen's comp is hard to beat!

Seniority

1 Molly O'Dell's follows strict guidelines regarding the assignment of shifts and duties, with the following exceptions.: Front-of-the-house employees willing to perform sexual favors may do so in exchange for prime shifts. It is the employee's responsibility to make sure the favors are performed for the manager in charge of scheduling. Management will not "pass on" favors to other managers.

2 Kitchen employees may perform as many favors as they like for the owner or scheduling manager, but it will make no difference. Kitchen employees will be scheduled for the most inconvenient hours possible. All kitchen employees will work the Saturday night/ Sunday morning split shift. Kitchen employees will not question unpaid overtime in exchange for management not questioning immigration or parole status.

Child Care

Only one child per employee may be left in the video game area at any given time. Do not bring three children to work, leave two at the bar, and claim you only brought one. If a member of management and an employee have children together, they may have a maximum of two children on the premises at any given time.

Fraternization

1 Other than the examples noted elsewhere in this manual, there will be no dating, sexual activity, or other relationships unnecessary to the job at hand between employees, management, customers, contractors, distributors, or inanimate objects on or off the premises of Molly O'Dell's.

2 If there is reason to suspect a sexual relationship between employees or managers, such situations may not be discussed among employees. Gossip will be considered insubordination and may be used as grounds for the assignment of restroom-cleaning duties.

3 All "special privileges" an employee may be receiving for unauthorized relations with management may be revoked at any time without explanation.

General Information

1 All policies in the employee manual are subject to change at any time at the discretion of management.

2 Employee rights are non-negotiable and may be revoked at any time without explanation.

3 Any employee who has a grievance with Molly O'Dell's management or policies must fill out the form at the back of this manual and file it in the bin in the manager's

office labeled "86."

If we all work together, we can make Molly O'Dell's an interesting and exciting place to work!

The Management

Illustration by Laura Kogonis

Utility
Anonymous with Moira Gentry

Q. Where are you from?

A. Belmont, Trinidad.

Q. How old are you?

A. 36.

Q. What is your job?

A. Utility—that's what they call it… anything they want you to do.

Q. Do you work for a company or for a building?

A. I work for Lincoln Center.

Q. For how long?

A. Five years.

Q. What is the worst thing about your job?

A. Filthy bathrooms. It's just… the building I'm cleaning is a building for employees only. So you can imagine when you come in and it's really filthy and you see feces on the floor. You're like, "Come on! There's no bums here!" Filthy.

Q. What is the best thing about your job?

A. This job is not for everyone. For me, I have that kind of rapport with my foreman, I can leave early, I can get time off if I need it.

Q. What was your worst day at work?

A. When someone was out, they called in sick, so I have to complete my routine and still assist in helping doing the routine of the person who was out sick. So I'm doing my job and a half.

Q. What's your best day at work?

A. The best is when it's a holiday and hardly anyone comes in and it's not that dirty. Easy day.

Q. If you could tell the world anything at all about your job, what would you say?

A. It's a job you can do… multitasking, you clean, you dust, you clean the computers, the offices, you vacuum, sweep and mop the floors. It's not a career. You don't want to stay 20 years at it. Not that kind of job. I've had other jobs where, you know, you're in a suit and tie and you're very clean. But here, the pay is better — strange to say, the pay is better.

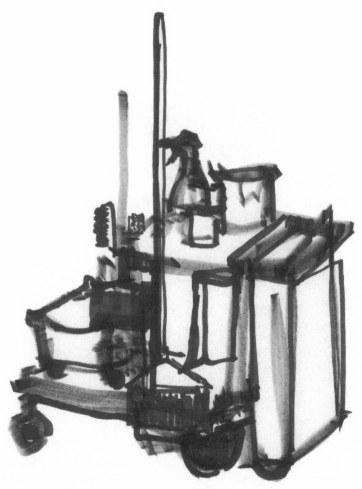

Illustration by Laura Kogonis

Dish Diary
Leah Ryan

April 4, 1979: Well, just as I was recovering from getting fired from Fay's Drugs, I got this call from Doreen. I mean I got fired on Thursday and she called on Saturday morning, not bad. She had heard about Fay's Drugs, how I "didn't work out" and everything. Fay's Drugs never came out and said exactly what the problem was. It was either my hair or my clothes or my attitude. Usually that's what it is. And it took me forever to get that job, because of the economy and due to the fact that I have no job experience and dropped out of high school and am sixteen and have blue hair. Doreen told me she could get me a job that would start right away. She told me listen, Emma, this job sucks so bad. It is the suckiest job you will ever have I HOPE. If you ever have a worse job, kill yourself. That's how bad it is. I asked her to tell me more. That's how desperate I was. She made me promise to keep looking, then she asked me if I could be there in an hour. Which I could.

Doreen isn't a dishwasher anymore. She got promoted and now she's a prep cook. Somehow, Saturday night, after working all day, Doreen ended up not only finding a new dishwasher (me) but training them too (me again). It was a crash course that only lasted about an hour, but she gave me lots of advice. She said, you are the dishwasher and you have the most important and the most horribly gross and disgusting job in the whole fucking kitchen! If the cooks give you a hot pot, they have to let you know otherwise you'll burn your fucking hand off! So tell them, say hey motherfucker, that pot's hot! What are you trying to do, kill me? We have to soak the silverware in this nasty chemical shit. Soilmaster. It's the law. One of the other dishwashers, Charley, likes to dump this shit into the pot sink. Fuck that, don't let him do it. He's lazy. He thinks it makes the pots easier to wash. He's full of fucking shit. The crap will burn your skin right fucking off. If the waitstaff throws the silver in the bucket and you get splashed with Soilmaster, tell them! Say, hey you fucking asshole, you tryin' to fucking blind me? That shit will burn my eyes right out of my head!

The dish area is about six feet long and about two feet wide. Doreen showed me how to use the dish machine and introduced me to

> That shit will burn my eyes right out of my head!

the cooks and to Rick, the general manager. If you ever have a problem, Doreen said, you just tell Rick. Rick's okay, Doreen said, and he's always here. Rick looked like he was about to drop dead. He was totally the wrong color, like gray. He had big bags under his eyes. This is Emma, Doreen said to the cooks. She's the new dishwasher! Be fucking nice to her, or she'll fucking quit! This job sucks! When she left, Nancy, who works the appetizer and salad station said to Rick that Doreen was too pretty to wash dishes. I guess they don't think that about me or they'd jump in and do it for me or something.

I was just starting to get the hang of it when Doreen came back. One of the cooks saw her come in and said, "We're out of chowder Mama." He didn't even say hello, plus he called her Mama which I couldn't believe he got away with. Doreen slapped her forehead so hard that she sort of lost her balance. She was kind of drunk. She yelled FUCKING CHOWDER MAMA. She grabbed me by the arm. Now you're going to learn to do chowder mama, she said. I was pretty confused. I followed her into the prep kitchen.

She took me into this storage room that was filled with huge cans. We started pulling them down. Clams, string beans, cream style corn, stewed tomatoes, cream of mushroom soup, potatoes, peas and carrots, chicken broth, a gallon jar of pickled onions, two quarts of clam juice. Then we got a big bucket. Doreen said, we make it in a fucking garbage can. Does that tell you anything? One by one we opened the cans and dumped them into the bucket. A glob of tomato splashed up into Doreen's hair and she yelled fuck! This job is so disgusting! Then she got a big paddle and mixed it all together. It was pretty gross. I asked her what they did with it. She told me that they scoop some out into a pot and add milk. They heat it up. That's it. She said, well, they add a little salt and pepper. People like it, she told me. They eat it. Next she had to show me how to clean up the kitchen, which was another fiasco full of yelling and grease and sweat. Forget being too pretty. Doreen hates that job. I guess I can understand why. And plus, how can you really have any respect for the customers who eat that crap?

Tuesday: Today I worked with Charley, who is the dishwasher that has been working there the longest. In the daytime, there is only one cook. His name is Ed and he's really short (like under 5 feet tall). He moves faster than anyone I have ever seen. When someone orders a burger well done, he yells "One hockey puck!" Charley, on the other hand, never shuts up and never does any work. He's one of those people who's really smart and really stupid at the same time. While I did the dishes, he told me all about the migration patterns of the Canada Goose (people who call them "Canadian" geese are just dead wrong, he says). Then I took a lunch break and he sat with me and told me everything he knew about Bonsai trees, which turned out to be quite a bit. When we (or I) went back to work, he told me about the time when he was five years old and his mother left him alone with a big bucket of Kentucky Fried Chicken and he ate it all. Ed said, Hey, Charley, why don't you tell her about the time she dropped you on your head? Charley ignored that but started to tell me about the time he broke both his arms while riding his bicycle. By this time it was 2:30 and Charley had been talking for five-and-a-half straight hours. Ed stopped cooking for a second and yelled, Hey, Charley shut the fuck up and do some work, will ya? Everybody got quiet for a second. Then, Charley's idea of getting to work was pouring the Soilmaster out of the silverware bin and into the sink. I didn't know what to do. I looked at the boxes piled up under the sink. The said "corrosive" and had a picture of a hand with something dripping onto it and there was a big hole in the hand.

But Charley was up to his elbows in it, the first work he's done all day. I asked him about it and he said not to worry about it. He said it was no big deal and would make the work go faster.

At 4 o'clock, the chef, Ron, came in, who I hadn't met yet because he was out sick on my first night. Ed said Ron gave himself food poisoning. I don't know if that's true or not. But Ron said "Welcome aboard!" and patted my back. He didn't look like a chef to me. He looked like a ten-year-old boy. He's only been with the restaurant for two months. They've had three chefs this year alone. Everyone talks behind Ron's back. Ron's specialty is supposedly Cajun food. Ed says he's been talking since he got there about this soup he makes called Gumbo Ya Ya. He hasn't actually made it yet though. You got to hand it to Ron that he didn't invent the chowder, or the chowder mama. Also, it wasn't his idea to call it "mama".

Thursday: I should have listened to Doreen! Tuesday night I woke up in the middle of the night and my hands and arms were all tingly. I turned on the light. I was all full of these red bumps and it burned like crazy. It's that fucking Soilmaster. Doreen said it would burn my skin right off, which it didn't do, but the rash is still there. I think I'm going to tell Rick that I think I know what I'm doing and I don't need Charley to train me anymore.

Ron made some Gumbo Ya Ya last night. He says it's almost there, but he hasn't quite perfected it yet. He asked me to try it, which is weird, because what the hell do I know about what Gumbo Ya Ya is supposed to taste like? Anyway, it didn't really seem to have much flavor. Actually, it had a dishwatery kind of taste to it. But I wasn't sure if it was just me. Of course I told him I thought it was really good. I showed Doreen my rash and she threw the potato she was peeling against the wall and yelled that fucking asshole Charley! This place fucking sucks! I think everybody at the restaurant is a little bit in love with Doreen.

I am really starting to get the hang of this dish thing now. There's a rhythm to it. In some ways I don't mind it, but my feet hurt and I feel like I never get rid of the smell.

Also, there's a few unwanted pets in the kitchen that I could do without. Like roaches the size of my fist. I have roaches at my apartment but they're small. Nothing like this. And also there's these rats that live in the river that are the size of tomcats and now and then they haul themselves onto the dock, I guess. That's what Ed said.

Saturday: Last night I worked with this guy who's name is supposedly "Ace." I want to find his W4 form so I can find out what his real name is. But anyway, even though he's only been there for a week longer than me, man is he fast! He says he's been washing dishes for 11 years. Wow. He says he's from North Carolina but he doesn't really have an accent.

Ron put the Gumbo Ya Ya on the line last night. He wants it to be a regular thing, like the chowder. But everybody's talking about how terrible the Gumbo Ya Ya is. I thought it was just that they don't like Ron, but then a customer actually sent it back. The waitress brought it up to the window and said "They hate this. They hate it." Ron kind of turned red and looked like he was controlling himself. Nancy looked at me and I looked at Ace but he didn't crack a smile because he was too busy being the best damn dishwasher that ever lived.

The people ended up getting chowder instead of the Gumbo Ya Ya, and I guess they were happy with it. That kind of bothers me. The Gumbo Ya Ya might be bad, but at least it's sort of....cooked. At least it's not just a bunch of cans thrown in a bucket. At least it doesn't have a mama.

Monday: Last night I showed up and Ed, who was just leaving, said, "Igor is sick." Igor is the garbage disposal. I asked Ed what was wrong with Igor, and Ed said, "Too much Gumbo Ya Ya". Sure enough, the kitchen was crawling with Roto Rooter men, and the pots and dishes were all piled up. Also the exterminator was there. You couldn't even move in the kitchen, so I went out on the dock and had a smoke. I think I might have seen a giant rat. It was big and it didn't look like a cat or a raccoon. I just saw the shape of it. I didn't want to get close. But maybe I'm just losing my mind.

Someone threw up all over the ladies' room floor, and rumor has it it looked just like Gumbo Ya Ya. I'm just glad it happened on the day shift, so Charley had to clean it up and not me. I've been at this job a little over a week, and I feel like I've been here for 20 years.

Wednesday: Yesterday I worked the day shift, and it was real slow, so I helped Doreen in the prep kitchen for a couple of hours. I found out she's been there two years and she's still making minimum wage. Which sucks. She taught me some stuff about using a knife. I'd like to learn to do what she does. She can slice mushrooms so fast you can barely see her knife moving. It's so cool. I also helped the pastry chef make roses for a wedding cake. I wouldn't mind learning that stuff either. One thing is for sure: I don't want to end up washing dishes for 11 years like Ace.

Someone at lunch sent back their Gumbo Ya Ya. Not everybody has the nerve to send it back. Lots of people just leave it sit and then the waitstaff gives it to me and I give it to Igor. Maybe that really is what made him sick. Ron is always talking about sanitation and delegation and all this management stuff. I think maybe he should learn to cook.

Monday: Saturday night the police came and took Ace away. His name is actually Frank. I knew it would turn out to be something like that. He was wanted in Ohio for assault, maybe even assault with a deadly weapon. Seems he held a Head Waiter hostage in the kitchen of some restaurant in Cleveland with a broken brandy snifter. Scary! Before I started this job, I didn't even know "snifter" was a word. Anyway, I guess that's what 11 years of washing dishes will do for your sanity. I'm glad they caught him in a way. I mean, what if I said something about his mother or something and he stabbed me with a fork? A fork full of Soilmaster? I also got a note in my paycheck. Everybody got one. It said that from now on you shouldn't punch in until you put your whites on. Everybody is pissed, because why would we be putting whites on if it wasn't a part of our job? I mean, isn't it a part of our job? Ed says something like this happens every few months when the owner sobers up for a couple days and freaks out about costs. Then he puts the squeeze on the managers. So Rick pretty much had to make this rule, even though he knew it was unfair. The whole thing just sucks, because people work pretty hard and there's like no hope of getting a raise. I figured out that the only person who's getting an okay deal in all this is Charley, because he just never does any work. I wish I could learn to be like that, but I know I can't. He never gets a raise, but neither do Ed and Doreen.

Oh, and I guess the owner really loves the Gumbo Ya Ya , so we have to serve it no matter what. I wonder how sober he was when he ate it.

Tuesday: Rick called an emergency staff meeting yesterday. Everyone was required to attend except Ron. This is the first time I've seen Rick really get upset. He said he didn't want to hear one more word about Gumbo Ya Ya, ever. No jokes, no remarks, no mention at all, unless absolutely necessary. We all looked at the floor. I think a lot of us were thinking about how hard this was going to be. Since Ace/Frank went to jail, I'm almost like the senior dishwasher, which is nuts, since I haven't even been working there three weeks. But Charley doesn't count. They just hired someone. I'm supposed to train him tonight. In the meantime, I'm on the schedule every single night until who knows when. Until the new guy gets trained, if he stays. The real drag is that I relieve Charley every day, and he always leaves the place a wreck. I come in to pots soaking in grease and Soilmaster, pots that could have been washed in five minutes. I have to reach down in to let the water out. Last night I got so sick of the smell, I looked down at my sneakers and saw the muck all over them; they're my only pair. I yelled This Job Fucking Sucks, and I really wanted someone to tell me I'm too pretty for this. I would have settled for being taken away in handcuffs.

But the thing is I'm on my own now, and it's not like I can quit. I have rent to pay and everything. I always look in the paper and ask around, but there are no jobs anywhere doing anything. At least I don't have to wear a stupid hat like at McDonalds, and I don't have to talk to customers. It's a lot harder than Fay's Drugs, but in a way it's better. The people are better. They're funny and they're good at what they do. Well, except for Ron. Charley is good at doing nothing, which is a kind of talent I guess.

I take my break around 9:30. It's busy tonight and I can only sit down for a few minutes. The guy working the line tonight is new. His name is John. He makes me a big fat cheeseburger. I eat, smoke a couple cigarettes and read the classifieds in the evening paper. I promised Doreen I'd keep looking, and I'm not going to let her down.

Illustration by Laura Kogonis

A Large Sparkling
Moira Gentry

"Thank you," the table said. "Next."

Marcie squinted past the lights to try and make out any possible facial expressions, but all she could see were looming shapes silhouetted against the door's backdrop. "Oh my gosh, okay, well, thank you," she trailed off.

"I hate auditioning," she thought. She walked across the avenue without looking and found herself face-to-face with an irate cab driver. "Tired of living?" he inquired. A truck blared behind him, and she jumped and he sped away. She walked into the café. "I need a new monologue," she said. "And a latte?"

The young man behind the counter smiled at her. "Hey, you left your Backstage here last time."

Marcie leaned her elbows on the counter and watched him steam the milk. "Why couldn't I have wanted to be a bond broker, or a car salesman, or something?" she asked.

"I know," he said. He had a tiny dumbbell through his septum and orange spikes all over his head. "This business is a bitch," he said.

"See, at least you're not bland," Marcie said. She put four sugars into her coffee. "I wish I wasn't bland."

"You're not bland," he said. "It just takes a long time."

Carlos sighed and shifted from one sore foot to the other. Now that the lunch rush, such as it was, was over, he had time to think. He hoped tonight's tips were better. Bills were piling up and Freddy was between jobs again.

"Water and bread on table five, please," Joe, the waiter, said. "Watch the floor, will you, Carlos? I'm going to grab a quick smoke, okay?"

"OK," Carlos said. Table five was two youngish theatrical-looking men. They smiled up at him with the awful charm of theater people. "Thank you so much," the younger one gushed. Carlos nodded. He didn't like to show his teeth. North Americans had such expensive looking teeth. He noticed that these two looked years older close up and that the older one was wearing a toupee, or a weave, or something. They kept smiling as he walked away. "They never stop," he thought. "They must get tired."

He gazed out the window. He thought about the guy he'd met at Cake last Tuesday night. They'd talked for a while because Carlos was waiting for Freddy, who was late, as usual. Carlos thought about the guy's funny hair, his pierced nose and his flood of conversation. He'd been nice.

The payphone in the hall rang. Joe, coming in just then, answered it. "Here, Papi, it's for you," he grinned and held out the phone. Carlos took it. "Yes?"

"Carlos," Freddy said. He sounded rushed. He had been sounding more and more rushed lately. He never seemed to get anywhere. "What time are you getting out of there?"

"I'm working a double," Carlos said. "I don't know. If it's not busy, then --"

"Again? I keep telling you, you don't need to work so much anymore. I got that job, you know, that's what I called to tell you, so we could go out and celebrate."

"What job?" Carlos thought about the jobs Freddy was always getting. None of them lasted.

"You remember, the night shift, the legal data entry thing. They're going to pay me seventeen fifty a hour, Carlito. An hour." Freddy laughed.

"When do you start?"

"God, Carlito, I don't know. Next week sometime. Try to get out of there early, okay? Maybe one day this week we can look for a better apartment."

"Maybe," Carlos said. He felt tired again. He shifted his weight. It didn't help.

"OK, babe, well I gotta run, OK?"

"Yeah, me too," Carlos said. He hung up the phone and stood there staring at it. He didn't want to look for another apartment with Freddy.

"Lover's quarrel?" Joe asked. Carlos shook his head and looked at the floor, his face hot.

"Well," Joe said, looking at his watch. "It's about time for the mountain to come to Mohammed, isn't it?"

Carlos looked out the window again. Every day, for the past week, an enormously fat woman with a pronounced limp had come into the restaurant. She always came in at four o'clock, and she always ordered the same thing: a double cappuccino and a piece of chocolate cake. The waiters and the bartenders and the managers laughed at her. Carlos liked her. He knew it was a terrible sin to be fat in the United States, but he thought she looked comfortable. She never grinned at him or gushed or talked down to him; in fact, she never talked to anybody. Except to order her coffee and cake, no one had ever heard her say one word. She didn't read a newspaper or a book either; she just sat there. She was serene, and she had miles of beautiful skin, fine-grained and clear as water.

The fat woman approached the door, and Carlos went to open it for her. She smiled up at him. He nodded politely.

He remembered the secondhand surfboard he'd bought in California, after he'd left Mexico. There had never been any time to use it. His roommates got on his case about how the apartment was too small to keep his ratty old board, and he had to get rid of it. One day, he put on his favorite shirt, took the board, and walked to beach. The white surfer boys yelled, "Hey dude, nice shirt, ugly board!" They laughed and watched him struggle out into the cold water. The light was strong and bright, the ocean sparkling. He couldn't catch a wave all day. The sky darkened, and he was about to give up when he found himself lifted and held on the curling water. He'd sold the board later that week.

Regina shifted the phone between her ear and her shoulder. The air in her apartment was blue with smoke, drifting around her Tony on its shelf. "But, honestly, Pat, it's really too much. Last night there was an ad on TV for a new movie, you know, with Jack forchrissakes Nicholson, I mean really. And Michael Caine, I swear to god, Michael Caine, you know, and some anonymous New Young Thing, they all look exactly alike, and it was being breathlessly pitched as a sexy new thriller, I mean, how on God's green earth are Jack Nicholson and Michael Caine still considered viable sex objects is so far beyond me I can't even tell you--" The phone started to fall off her shoulder. She settled it against her ear again to hear Pat saying, "Well, it's Jack Nicholson, you know--"

"Yes, goddammit, I am perfectly aware, Pat, that's what I'm saying. I mean, look, you don't see anybody selling Shirley Maclaine, for godsakes, or, god, I don't know, Susan goddam Sarandon as sex objects. Susan's years younger than Jack, eons younger, but she gets to play, you know, the mother, or a nun, for chrissakes, or a goddam alcoholic lawyer for some brat --"

"She gets a lot of work," Pat said quietly.

Regina took a deep breath. She stretched out her hand so she could glare more freely at her recent manicure. She noticed with dread that her wrists were even bonier than they had been last week. "Okay. Fine. Look, Patty, my old darling, did those people get back to you about my reading?"

There was a pause. Regina felt her stomach begin to burn again. Stress, the doctor said. She'd thought she had ulcers. "If I lose any more weight," she thought desperately.

Pat sighed heavily into her ear. "Well, my dear Regina, it's like this. They really want someone, you know, a little, younger."

"Oh god," Regina said. She lit another cigarette. Less smoking, the doctor had said. Try some of that gum.

"Hedda Gabler's a young woman," Pat said.

"But, Pat, It's my part, I've played it before, I know it, I look it, I gave a beautiful reading, those bastards had tears in their eyes, Pat, actual goddam tears —you know, 'I'm burning your child, I'm burning your child, from now on I will be quiet'--"

"Well, listen, I think I've got a Tide commercial for you and <u>General Hospital</u> called back about a day gig and --"

"You didn't, by any chance, happen to hear anything about that Off-Broadway Macbeth thing, did you? With that young director the Voice went on and on about?"

"Well, no. But maybe --"

"All right, Pat," Regina said. "I've got to run now. Thank you."

"I'll call you about the Tide thing, then." Pat sounded tired.

"Yes, of course," Regina said. "Thank you so much." She hung up, took a long drag on her cigarette, and then stubbed it out. "From now on," she thought, staring at the ashtray, "I will be quiet."

"Late again," the manager said in a bored tone of voice.

"I know, I know. I'm really sorry, all right?" Marcie threw off her coat and tied on her apron. She looked around vaguely and started to walk toward the bar, then suddenly switched back and went toward the dining room, bumping into Milos, the other waiter, nearly knocking him over. "Oh my gosh, Milos," she said breathlessly, "are you all right? I'm really, really sorry. I had yet another lousy audition today and --"

"Please get out of my way," Milos said. He went to the bar and poured himself a Coke.

"Maybe if you punched in?" the manager suggested.

"Oh my gosh," Marcie said. "I keep forgetting."

The manager shook his head and went back to his inventory. "Pre-meal meeting in 10 minutes, everybody," he said without looking up. "Steam your glasses. No spots on the silverware, either. I'll be checking."

Marcie ran downstairs and stood there looking for her time card. "It's never where I left it," she informed the time clock. "Hey, honey," she called to Eduardo, the prep cook. He blew her a kiss. "Bonita," he smiled at her. "Mi amor."

Back upstairs, Joe, Milos and Luis, the food runner, sat wiping menus. "She's still here," Joe said. He gestured with his chin toward the fat lady. "She's been sitting here since four. I think she's waiting for something."

"Yeah," said Milos. "A forklift."

"You're so mean," Marcie said. She sat down and Luis shoved a pile of menus toward her.

"A coronary thrombosis," Joe said. "At least she tips for the time she sits here and not on what she orders."

"Make me an espresso," Milos told Marcie. "A short one."

"No way."

"A short one. Come on."

"Oh my gosh," Marcie said. She put down the menu she was wiping and went to the machine. "Make me a chamomile tea?" Joe called. "Please?"

"Hey Carlito," she said. He nodded at her and went back to wiping silverware.

Carlos took the silverware out to the waiter's station and began putting it away. He thought that it might be fun to have just one little weekend affair. With someone nice, like that guy at Cake. Someone not in a big rush to nowhere. "I'll probably never see him again, though," Carlos thought. "I wish I'd gotten his number."

He looked up, and the fat lady was looking in his direction. He smiled at her, not caring about his teeth. She smiled back. He went back to polish more silverware.

"All right everybody," the manager said. "The soup is potato leek, chicken stock, this is not a vegetarian soup, fish is grilled sea bass with asparagus and roasted potatoes, the vegetable is garlic mashed potatoes. Eighty-six pork chops and Sierra Nevada. And, as I'm sure you've all heard, the State in its infinite wisdom has raised waiter's hourly salary from 2.17 to 2.37 per hour." He stopped and waited for cries of gratitude from the assembled waiters, food runners and busboys. They stared at the floor. He sighed. "So. I really need those check averages up, and sell bottled water. And... Marcie." She looked up. "Why can't you sell bottled water?" he asked her. "You have the lowest check averages of any waiter in this restaurant."

Marcie took a deep breath. "The thing is? I'm not intimidating. And you know I upsell like crazy, but they're not intimidated by me and so, if they want to be cheap, which they do, they see me coming and they're all like, 'Well we can be as cheap as we want,' and I say, can I get you a cocktail or a glass of wine while you look at the menu, and they're all, 'no we just want water,' and I say, Sparkling? Or non-sparkling? And also if I hear that joke one more time, the 'We'll just have the Guiliani special ha ha ha,' I will die, I'm like, Oh, that's funny. That's a funny joke which I only hear about

165

a million times a day, and -"

"Just please sell some bottled water, OK? Please?" He walked away.

"OKAY." Marcie fell into the chair.

Luis stood and tied on his apron. "If you sell more," he told Marcie, "we all get better tips." He went into the kitchen to prep garnishes.

"Two-Thirty-Seven an hour?" Joe said. "How will I ever manage to spend it all?"

Milos put four sugars into his coffee. "Your voice is so annoying," he said to Marcie. "Yap yap yap, like a little dog."

"You're so sinister," Marcie told him.

"I don't know," Joe said. "It's a heavy responsibility, that kind of wealth."

"Thanks for the espresso," Milos told Marcie.

"Why did you pour coffee all over that old guy at table seven the other day?" Joe asked her.

"It was snowing," Marcie said.

"And?"

"It was really pretty, and I was looking at it, and then I started to space out--"

"Started," Milos muttered.

"And so I was refilling his coffee cup, you know, only I forgot, and next thing I know, he's waving his arms and shouting, and I look down and there's this lake of coffee--"

"Actors. Fucking actors," Milos said. "You're the reason the fuckers who come here tip so shitty." He gathered up the menus to put away in the host's station. "Time to get to work."

"She's still here," Joe said, looking over at the fat lady. "Unbelievable. Come on, let's go steam glasses."

"I have to get out of this apartment," Regina thought. "Maybe I'll go drink myself into a stupor." She threw on her furs and fixed her lipstick in the hall mirror. In the elevator she wondered again about the O'Brien audition. "Damn," she thought. Her stomach burned. "Of course I had to just throw it away. Of course I'm just casual about an Off-Broadway experimental Shakespeare thing which screams Obie, with a rising young director that even the bloody Times called refreshing. Oh god. Commercials. Soap opera dailies."

She posed in the restaurant doorway for the shortest of beats before she swept up to the bar and sat regally down in her usual spot. "Lighting," she thought. "Timing." She examined at her reflection in the mirror behind the bar. "My lift looks goddamn good in this light. I don't look a day over thirty. Oh god."

Sully, the bartender, leaned over the bar to her. "You're looking ravishing as always tonight, darlin'." He flashed his most killing smile.

"Don't try to upstage me, you little bastard," she thought. She smiled magnificently. "A Perfect Rob Roy," she told him in her thrilling, get-'em-in-the-back-row, husky murmur. "Black Label, please."

Marcie approached the table with her biggest smile. "Hi, folks, how are you this evening?"

They looked up at her. "Good," they said. "How are you?"

"I'm good," Marcie lied. "Can I get you a cocktail or a glass of wine while you look at the menu?"

They looked at the wine menu. "I'll just have water,"

said one, and then the rest nodded their heads.

"Sparkling, or non-sparkling?" Marcie asked desperately.

"Just the Guiliani special," they all laughed.

"Excuse me?" Marcie asked. She wanted to make them spell it out, even if she did have to laugh for a better tip.

"Tap water," the table said. "New York City tap water. Get it?"

Marcie forced a laugh. Her face hurt.

"With lemon," the woman told her.

"Oh, absolutely," Marcie said.

"Carlos, por favor, four tap waters on table fifty one. I'll get the lemon."

He nodded.

Luis was at the bar, filling little buckets with freshly cut lemons and limes. "Be careful about your table numbers," he told her as she put lemon wedges around the rim of a rocks glass. "Last night, I have to bring entrees to the wrong table again. This is another reason why our tips suck."

Marcie nodded. Her section was rapidly filling.

"Hello, ladies, how are you this evening?" This table was two older women.

"Can I get you a glass of a wine or a cocktail while you look at the --"

"Water," they said.

"Sparkling, or non --"

"Tap water," they told her severely. "No ice."

"How are the roasted market vegetables prepared?" asked one. "Are they fried? Because I can't eat them if they're fried. I'm on a special diet, you know, and I simply cannot eat anything fried. Are they fried?"

Marcie looked around. Her section was full of tables she hadn't gotten to yet and the manager was giving her that look again.

She took a deep breath. "They would be, um, roasted," and she smiled some more.

"Oh, then they're not fried," said the lady. "Are you sure they're not fried?"

"I'll give you a few minutes with the menu," Marcie said politely.

"Just bring us two house salads," the lady on the special diet told her. "With the dressing on the side."

Steven walked into the restaurant and stood uncertainly in the doorway. The manager bustled up. "How many?"

"Well-"

"Reservations?"

"Well no, I don't want a table. Actually, I-"

"The bar is right back there." He looked at Steven's orange spikes and the miniature dumbbell through his nose. "Sir."

"Well, okay. Great," said Steven. "Thanks." He walked to the bar, looking around him.

"Hey," Marcie said. "It's the Not Bland Guy."

"Yeah, I-"

"See?" Marcie said. "You don't remember me."

"No," Steven said. "I remember you. Actually I remember your voice."

"Oh my gosh," Marcie said. "My voice. They keep sending me out on auditions for teenage roles. Last time I was on stage I played a 15-year-old. I wish I could get voice-over work, then it might be of some use."

"It's kind of cute, actually. I was looking for someone, I think he works here, Carlos?"

"Oh, Carlos. He's right over there."

"Marcie, stay in your section please," the manager said. "I got a cocktail order on table 21. And a large sparkling." He walked to the bar.

"Oh my gosh. Thank you." She turned to Steven. "He's not bland. He's intimidating. They're afraid to ask him for tap water. Okay, bye."

"Bye," Steven said.

"Hey, folks, how are you this evening?"

"Fine," the table said. The restaurant clattered and hummed around her.

Marcie took another deep breath. Her feet ached. "Can I get you a cocktail or a glass of wine while you–"

"We just want water," the table said.

"How about a nice bottle of mineral water with lemon or lime?"

"Oh," said one. "I'd love some lemon with mine."

"But tap water's fine," said another.

"All right, then," Marcie said. A deep despair settled on her.

"I want lime with mine," said another one. Marcie nodded, smiling wildly.

Regina sipped her drink and checked her face in the mirror again. She noticed some commotion behind her, and she saw Sully's lips quirk as if he were trying not to laugh. She looked over her shoulder and the fattest woman she had ever seen walked by Regina on her way to the bathroom. "My god," thought Regina, "how strictly mountainous. And a limp." Regina watched the fat lady's rolling walk.

She thought of the time she had gone on a two-week sailing trip around the coast of Maine. The boat had rocked like the fat lady's walk, on the water, and Regina remembered how well she'd slept at night on the boat. "I didn't even want to smoke," she thought. "My stomach didn't hurt. Food tasted good. Oh, god." She lit another cigarette and motioned to Sully. "Same again, please." Regina remembered that the bathroom door was heavy and would be hard for someone with a cane to manage. She slipped off the barstool and went to hold the door. The fat lady looked up at Regina and Regina flashed her luminous smile.

The fat lady smiled back.

"Hello, folks, how are you?"

"Fine," the table said. "And you?"

"Oh, fine," Marcie smiled some more.

"Do you have coffee drinks?"

"Oh, yes," Marcie said hopefully. "Espresso, cappuccino, we also have a wide selection of teas--"

"Can I get a cuppachino with no milk?" said one.

"Well, you know," Marcie said. The manager was in her section at another table she hadn't gotten to yet. "No."

"Well what flavors do you have?" asked another.

"I beg your pardon?" Marcie said. The manager was bringing a bottle of Jordan and a large sparkling to her table.

"Vanilla, hazelnut, you know," the person looked around at the others with a Can-You-Believe-This-Dumb-Chick look.

"Oh, I'm sorry, we have nothing like that. We have really good Italian espresso."

"I want plain regular coffee."

"I want water," said another. "Plain regular water." The table laughed.

Carlos saw Steven standing there and dropped the tray of silverware. Steven rushed over to help him pick it up. "Hi," Steven said.

"Hi," said Carlos.

"Listen, I know you're busy and I hope you don't mind me coming in here like this but I wanted to ask you something and I actually didn't know how to get in touch with you and I remembered, you know, at Cake? We met? You said you worked here. So anyway, to make a long story short, I've written a script, and we're going into production next week, and I was thinking that there's a part for you. If you want."

Carlos stared at him. "A part?"

"Oh, hey, it's not—I mean you wouldn't be playing a, you know, drug dealer, or a criminal or anything, it's not like that, actually."

"I'm not an actor," Carlos said.

"Yeah, well, actually, that's okay, see, because we're sorta using real people anyway."

"I don't think I could go on a stage--"

"What—oh right. No. It's a movie actually, a small independent film, you know, young gay men in Chelsea, a romantic comedy, and it would be really easy and fun. It won't take up much of your time, a weekend or so. I know you have to get back to work now, but here's my card. Give me a call, okay?"

"Excuse me," Carlos said. The card felt warm in his hand. "What is the part?"

"Um, well, actually you would play my lover. Do you think that would be okay?"

There was a pause.

"I think I could do that," Carlos told the tray.

"Great! Well, give me a call, okay?"

Carlos stood there after Steven left, smiling at the silverware.

"Hey, folks, how are you this evening?" This table was four suits. They stared at her.

"Can I get you a cocktail or a beer while--"

172

"Do you have any specials?" said one.

"Yes, our soup this evening is potato leek--"

They were laughing. "Excuse me?" Marcie said. "Is something funny?"

"Is that your real voice?" said one.

"I beg your pardon?"

"That can't be your real voice," said another.

"You sound like a cartoon character," said a third.

"I'll just give you a few minutes with the menu," Marcie said.

"No, no," the table said. "We're in a hurry. We'll order now. We'll make it easy for you, we're all having the pork chops."

"Oh my gosh," Marcie said. "I'm really sorry, I'm really really-- but we're out. I mean, we don't have the pork chops tonight."

"That sucks," he said. "Are you sure?"

Marcie nodded.

"Well, I don't know, I guess steak for me, medium."

"I'll have the grilled salmon," said another.

"How would you like that cooked, sir?"

"Grilled," he said very patiently.

"No, sir, I mean, rare, medium--"

"Pink," he said.

Marcie smiled nodded some more. She felt as if her head would fall off. She turned to the next suit.

"I'll have the steak. Medium."

"Me too," the last suit said.

Marcie leaned over to collect the menus. "Would you care for a salad or a soup to start with? I can recommend the soup," she said. "Or a nice pasta dish to share--"

"Just put that order in, will ya?" the table said. "We're in a hurry."

"Your check averages stink," the manager told her as she put the order into the computer. "You really need to raise those check averages."

Marcie nodded. Another table was flagging her. "And no mistakes," the manager said.

"Hi, folks, can I get you a cocktail--"

"I want a White Zinfandel," said the young woman.

"I'm sorry, ma'am, we don't have--"

Luis elbowed Marcie's back on his way by. He held two salads.

Marcie gently turned the wine list so the young woman could read it. "We have a very nice Pinot Grigio by the glass, and a Riesling--"

"Give me a Diet Coke," the young woman said without looking at the wine list.

"I'll take a Bud Light," her date said. "And can we order? We have to catch a movie in, like," he looked at his watch, "20 minutes."

"Light and a Diet, please, Sully," she said. She shifted from one foot to the other. It didn't help.

"Be right with ya, darlin'," he said.

Luis hissed "wrong table" at her and then vanished into the kitchen. She stared after him.

A man sitting at the bar next to the service station leaned toward her. "What're ya doing later, sweetheart?"

"Um, sidework," Marcie said and took her drinks to the table. Luis came out of the kitchen with two salads on one arm and two entress on the other.

The table the manager had brought the Jordan to wanted another. She ran back to the bar. "Bottle of Jordan, please," she called.

"Ooh," Sully said.

"And can I borrow your wine key please mine broke–"

"No," the man at the bar told her. "I mean after work."

"Going home. Alone," Marcie said. "Thanks, Sully." The coffee table flagged for their check.

"Return it, darlin', or die." Sully handed her the wine key.

She dropped the check on the table. "Thank you so much, folks," she said. One handed her his credit card and she took it to the computer.

"She's still here," Joe said. He nodded toward the fat lady. "Hurry up, I need to get in there."

Marcie opened the bottle of Jordan, poured a taste in the glass nearest the man she thought had ordered it, and waited. He was yelling into his cell phone. Marcie shifted her weight nervously. The table ignored her. Finally he waved his hand impatiently at her and poured out the wine himself, still yelling into his phone. Every water glass in her section was empty.

"Carlos, please, please can you refill waters in my section, please," she said.

"What table?" he asked her. He had a dazed, happy look.

"No, no," she told him. "My gosh, Carlos. Please refill water glasses. They're already on the tables. Refills everywhere, okay?"

"OK," Carlos said.

"Don't ya want some company?" the man at the bar leered at her.

The date table flagged for their check.

"No, thank you," Marcie told the man. "Here's your wine key back, Sully." She rang up the check.

The lady on the special diet flagged her. Marcie dropped the check on the date table and went over to the lady. "Yes, Ma'am?"

"My salad is gritty," the lady said. "And I told you, I wanted my dressing on the side."

"Yes, Ma'am." Marcie picked up the salad plate and took it to the manager. "Gritty," she told him.

"What table?"

"Table one hundred and two," Marcie told him.

He went to the computer and Marcie went to pick up the money from the date table.

"Change, please, Sully," she called.

"Why don't you and me go out for a little drink after work," the man at the bar said. "I know this place, this real nice little place--"

"I'm sorry, sir," Marcie said. "I'm afraid that, owing to a death in my family, I will be unavailable for any social events for the rest of all eternity."

"Here ya go, darlin'," Sully said.

"What table was that you said?" asked the manager.

"One hundred and one. No, two."

"Well, that's interesting," said the manager. "That's fascinating. Because you rang up the salads for table one hundred and two under table one hundred and one. And where does this glass of wine belong, exactly?"

Marcie looked at the check. "A glass of Sangiovese?"

The tap water with lemon and lime table was flagging her. Luis sped by with four entree plates lined up on one arm and two held in his other hand. He gave her a dirty look.

"Um, I have no idea," Marcie said. The manager shook his head.

"Can I get you folks a cappuccino, espresso?" She started to clear the table and Carlos came and took all the plates. She put dessert menus on the table.

"Do you have brewed decaf?" said one.

"Yes," Marcie said. The manager flagged her. Her feet hurt all the way to her shoulders. "We also have decaf espresso, decaf cappuccino--"

"Regular decaf for me. Do you have skim milk?"

"Um, no, I'm sorry--"

"Lowfat?"

"Well, no."

"Nothing for me then. We'll just take the check."

"Would you like a piece of chocolate cake or any sorbet--"

"The check," the table said.

Regina turned to see Pat breathlessly hoisting his plump behind up onto the stool next to her.

"What on earth--"

He waved at her with one hand and grabbed a bar napkin and delicately patted his brow with the other.

"Oh dear," he panted. "My dear Regina, I'm so glad I found you. Oh my dear, the most amazing thing, I couldn't believe it, and your doorman said I might find you here, and then the most irate cabbie--"

Regina motioned to Sully to pour the same for Pat. "Patty, my old darling, please try to be calm, here, have a sip of this before you completely start to hemorrhage, for chrissakes."

"Well," Pat gestured largely at Sully not to make the drink. "Well. After I hung up with you, right after, the phone rang and who do you think it was?"

Regina lit a cigarette and exhaled into his face. "Less with the dramatics, please, darling. I believe that's my department--"

Pat threw his shoulders back triumphantly. "Rachel O'Brien, that's who."

"Oh god, that young director, oh, Pat--"

"Yes, and they're starting rehearsals next week, and you're Lady Macbeth and she said they loved your reading and you're perfect and she said she especially loved how you threw it away and--"

"'Wash your hands, put on your nightgown,'" Regina intoned. Sully looked over, startled. "'Look not so pale! What's done is done.'" She grabbed Pat and planted a kiss on his cheek, and sat back admiring the red imprint she'd left.

Pat leaned over the bar to Sully and very grandly said, "a bottle of Veuve Cliquot, please, darling."

The suits paid in cash and Marcie took the money to the bar.

"Sully?" He wasn't there.

"I'll get it," the manager said. He rang up the check and shook his head over the size of the tip before he put it into the tip box.

"That's sad, sweetheart, that's real sad," the man at the bar said. "Who died?"

"You make one more mistake and--" the manager drew his finger across his throat with a hissing sound.

"Me," Marcie told the man. "Me." The manager handed her the change.

"You just got sat again," he told her. "Hurry up."

Milos came up to the bar. "I got a cocktail order on your new table," he told Marcie. "Two Gold margaritas up, salt, and a large sparkling."

"Oh my gosh," Marcie said. She stood there. Her feet felt as if some small important bones were broken.

"Please get out of my way," Milos said. He poured himself a Coke.

"Listen," the manager said. "Since Milos covered that, why don't you go to table three and see if you can't get her out of here."

Table three was the fat lady with the limp. "OK," Marcie said.

Regina flagged Sully. "What can I getcha, darlin'?" he said. The manager looked over.

"Are there any tables available?" she asked. "We've decided to eat dinner."

"We have?" Pat said.

The manager bustled up and handed them menus. "If you don't mind a wait," he told Regina. "Otherwise Sully will be happy to serve you at the bar."

Sully leaned over and stage-whispered, "Try the sea bass, darlin'. It's to die for."

"Fine," Regina said and grabbed Pat's menu and handed both back to the manager. "Two, please. And the potato leek soup to start."

Pat stared at her.

She patted his hand. "Just a little something," she murmured into his astonished face. "To keep our strength up."

"Um, excuse me, Ma'am?" Marcie leaned on the empty chair, trying to take some weight off her feet, and smiled at the fat lady. "Can I get you anything?"

"Well, let's see," the fat lady said. Her voice was clear and gentle. "What's your name, my dear?"

"Marcie," Marcie said. "Well, actually, it's Marcella, my mom called me after a great aunt, well, not the aunt, you know, a character in a novel. I mean, my mom's aunt wrote this book and so I was named after the title character because the book won the Pulitzer."

"I see. You're very busy tonight?"

"Well no, it's not so much that- it's just that, I don't know, I can't seem to concentrate and I keep making stupid mistakes and Milos is so fast and I can't even get anyone to buy bottled water, you know?"

"I see," said the fat lady.

"I mean, my gosh, I'm sorry, I can't imagine why

I just told you all that but we didn't even think you ever said anything, you know, because you never say anything, you know?"

"Is your family very literary, my dear?"

Marcie nodded, looking at the fat lady. She hadn't really looked at anyone's face in a long time. "I can't ever see their faces," she thought. "I just smile and smile and never look."

"Yes," Marcie said. "Very goddam literary. You know? My grandfather was a professor at Harvard and my father was an editor at Simon and Schuster and my great-aunt wrote books and my grandfather wrote books and people wrote books about them and it was all, you know, prizes and conferences and secret affairs and summers in Vermont and swimming in the lake and, and, going fishing--"

"I see."

"And now I'm here." Her face felt rested, and she realized it was because she wasn't smiling. "What a relief," she thought.

"And now I'm here," she went on, "and I've been doing this for like about a million years and I'm still not good at it and it makes me feel stupid and I thought I would be an actor, you know? But that doesn't seem to be working either. So, and so—that's that. Can I get you anything?"

"I think I'll just take my check, Marcella," the fat lady said. "I wish you all the luck in the world, my dear. I'm sure it will all work out for you very soon."

"Oh," Marcie said. "Oh, thank you."

Marcie rang up the fat lady's check. "You have tables," the manager said.

"I know," Marcie told him. The check printed out. She walked away and placed the check on the fat lady's table. "Thank you, Ma'am."

"You're welcome, my dear," the fat lady said.

"What can I get you?" Marcie asked the table. She still wasn't smiling.

"Do you have mineral water?" asked one. "Sparkling?"

"Yes," Marcie said. "In fact we do."

"Great. Well, a bottle of that, no fruit, please, and we'll all start with a salad each, then we'll share some pasta, what's good?"

"The ravioli," Marcie said, dumbfounded.

"OK, then a ravioli, no, two, to share, then I'll have the rack of lamb, medium."

Marcie turned to the next one. "I'll have the sea bass."

"And I'll take the veal chop."

"The prime rib for me, rare, all right? Still cold inside, all right? Still mooing. Just spank it and bring it on out here, all right?"

"All right," Marcie said. "Thank you very much."

"Thank you," the table said. "Oh, and a bottle of Pinot Gris, for now, and we'll decide on a red for later."

"Oh my gosh," Marcie thought. She put the order into the computer and went to the bar. "A large sparkling, please, Sully, and a bottle of Pinot Gris," she said importantly.

"Listen sweetheart," the man at the bar told her, "I'm real sorry to hassle you like that. I don't know what I was thinking. I'm 50 years old and unhealthy and bald and lonely and I drink too goddam much, excuse my language, and you really handled it very well, and I'll just go away now and never bother you ever again."

Marcie stared at him. He handed Sully a $20 tip and got his coat and left. Marcie turned back to Sully. "And I'll need to borrow your wine key again?"

"Keep it," said Sully, handing her the wine key. "There's like five of 'em back here."

Marcie stood, stunned. The manager came up and handed her the check with the unaccounted for glass of Sangiovese. "Did you figure this out?" he asked her. Marcie shook her head. She glanced over at the fat lady, who was beginning the lengthy process of getting out of her chair. Sully leaned over the bar to look at the check.

"Oh, that," Sully said. "I put that on there. They waved me over, and you looked kinda busy, darlin', so I just trotted it out to 'em."

"Oh, yes, of course," Marcie said. The fat lady was almost out of her chair. The manager handed Marcie the check. "Go drop it then," he told her.

Marcie brought the large sparkling and the Pinot Gris to the table and opened the wine for them. She poured a taste for the one who'd ordered it. He swirled it, took a sip and nodded up at her. She poured it around. "This is good," he said. "We'll take another, when you get a minute, please."

"My pleasure," Marcie said. The fat lady was putting her coat on.

Luis came up to the table with four salad plates on his arm. "Nice one," he whispered to her as he served them.

"Here you go, ladies." Marcie put the check on the Sangiovese table.

"You have quite a good wine list here," one said, handing her a pile of money. "Keep the change."

"Listen, I was wondering," said the other. "Do you do voice-over work?"

"I wish," Marcie told her. The lady on the special diet with the gritty salad flagged her. "Well, goodnight."

She walked slowly over to the other table.

"Check, please," the lady told Marcie. "The service was terrible, the salad was uneatable, and the music was too loud. I'm going to have to speak with the manager."

"Also there's a draft," said the other one.

The Sangiovese women were leaving. As Carlos bused their table, they stood talking to him and one handed him something. On their way out the door, they waved and Marcie waved back.

"I see, Ma'am," Marcie told the special diet lady, without smiling. She put their check on the table and walked to the bar for the second Pinot Gris.

Carlos came up to her, wiping his hands on his apron. "A table left a business card for you." He took it out of his pocket.

"Oh my gosh," Marcie said. "Another one?"

"Not this time," Carlos said. "Look."

Marcie looked at the card. Meredith Allen, Voice Over Casting.

Carlos smiled at her. "She said for you to call her Monday morning."

The fat lady was leaving, leaning heavily on her cane as she undulated toward the door. Marcie took the card from Carlos and ran to hold the door for her.

"Thank you, my dear," the fat lady said.

"Listen," Marcie said. "Are you—I mean, do you…" She trailed off. Behind her the restaurant clattered and hummed. She took a deep breath.

"Yes, my dear?"

"Oh," Marcie said. "Nothing. Have a nice night."

The fat lady smiled.

Her table flagged Marcie for another bottle of mineral water and she went back on the floor.

Illustration by Laura Kogonis

Driving It Up and Down
Anonymous with Moira Gentry

Q. Where are you from?

A. Dominican Republic.

Q. How old are you?

A. Twenty-seven.

Q. What is your job?

A. Elevator man. I drive a manual elevator. I drive it up and down. I take people to their floors. I have to sort their mail, take in their dry cleaning, wipe their ass... you know.

Q. Totally. How long have you been working at this job?

A. Seven years.

Q. What is the worst thing about your job?

A. A lot of times they don't see you as a person, you know. We don't wear costumes or whatever, uniforms —but they still see you as a uniform... a thing. Few people say hello. They're so fake too. They're not genuine.

Q. How so?

A. Because at times they're... they acknowledge you in the building, say "hello," "get my mail," but once you get outside, they walk right by you, like they didn't just see you five minutes ago. I get this a lot because I live right in the neighborhood.

Q. What is the best thing about your job?

A. The best thing is when real genuine people do move into the building. They're nice, they talk to you like you're a person. They ask you about your family. Actually concerned. In a building of 75 apartments there's maybe four or five apartments who see you as a person. And I won't even talk about the management. They're the worst.

Anything to raise the rent, anything to cut corners.

Q. What was your worst day at work?

A. One time, this older lady, she was upset at me, I heard about it from her friend, because I would call her by her first name instead of calling her Miss so and so. That really hurt me, because I thought we were friends. Maybe six months later, she had a heart attack and she couldn't move and she needed me to help her. Then she didn't mind if I called her by her first name. She needed me so much.

Q. What was your best day at work?

A. I think it's when the super actually started taking me seriously about replacing him when he retires. He started teaching me tricks of the trade: how to take care of the boiler, stuff like that.

Q. If you could tell the world anything at all about your job, what would you say?

A. I feel like saying there are a lot of fake-ass people… Dealing with tenants, they give you a hard time but there are those who don't see you as a lower status person. They see you as a person — they make up for the others.

Illustration by Laura Kogonis

Illustration by Laura Kogonis

Don't Kill the Messenger
Christopher Seifert (with Leah Ryan)

In 1990, I got my first bike messenger job. I got lost a lot. I eventually figured my way around. It was fun, because I already loved riding my bike, and now I was learning how to deal with traffic, and with pedestrians, and really getting to know my way around. I think that still, all this time later, my sense of direction was honed at that job, and it's still with me.

I believed I was getting pretty good at the job. Then one day, I think it was in November, I was riding down Beacon Street, down the hill, across Tremont Street, onto School Street, and I noticed that traffic was stopping. There was a 10-wheel truck that came to a stop right in front of me. I swung around to the right of him and kept my speed alongside of the truck and the parked cars. As I was just about to come alongside the passenger door, I noticed three women crossing the street, talking and eating bagels and drinking coffee. There was no time to stop. I was going to run all three of them over with my bicycle. I was freaked out, of course, and I did what was just natural -- I cut the handle-bars all the way to the right. I went over the bars and was airborne. I shoulder to shoulder checked the first woman, and like dominoes, all three went down and then I landed in front of the third woman. What I most remember seeing was a bagel flying through the air

and the lettuce and tomato and bagel all separating, and then I hit the road.

Well, of course I had created quite a scene. The women, rightfully so, were absolutely bullshit with me, the driver of the truck had to get out and threaten me, I had to get my bike and straighten it out a bit, all while everyone was screaming at me. Then, I realized that they were not in the crosswalk that was about 20 yards ahead of them. Well, we all had a lot of screaming, and I gave up my name and the company I worked for (I was seriously reprimanded and nearly lost my job) and finally rode away a little weary. The bagel, tomato, and lettuce separating is still my strongest memory of that incident, and the women did try and bring some

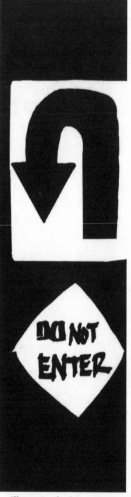

Illustration by Laura Kogonis

legal action against my company. I had to go out to the office and give a statement to a lawyer, and my realization that they were not in the crosswalk saved the company a huge lawsuit.

Soon after that I was riding into Boston from Southie, straight down what used to be Summer Street, and that bridge that is now gone (good riddance, as it was brutal on a bike and didn't seem too safe). I was thinking about this new law that had been passed about bike messengers needing to be licensed, since I wasn't at that time. They had just passed this bill, and no, I don't think it was because of my hitting those women, but I do wonder. I had heard about many other accidents and in fact, one death. A messenger running a red light had been struck and went through the windshield. But there are many, many other stories.

So anyway, I'm riding right down Summer Street and talking to my dispatcher when this big freaking Lincoln Town Car's door swings open almost right into me, but my front wheel (traveling around 17 to18 miles per hour) slides into the door pushing it open and then it won't open anymore.

So I wake up. I guess I had been out for a few minutes there, and I'm just realizing what had happened when I hear this guy screaming, "What the FUCK!!!" I get to my feet and, still reeling a little bit, grab my bike. It was like an accordion, and the front wheel was mangled at a 90- degree angle. The bike is not being ridden ever again. That taken in stock, I turn my attention to the guy, who is still screaming at me. I look at the car door that he's tugging on and shouting at me. The door, much like the bike, is never going to be a working door again. The driver is irate with me. I'm not too pleased with him at this time, and we are making a scene. A cop on traffic duty (nearby they are working on the bridge again, no surprise) ambles over to us, I think t keep us from going to blows with each other.

He takes in the scene and as he's doing this my walkie-talkie is up to full volume. It squelches "131, you all right? 131, where are you, 131 come in please." I immediately turn it off. "You're a messenger!" is now what the guy is screaming at me. "You're supposed to be licensed and wearing a vest! Where's your vest?" This new bill had in it that messengers need to wear this fluorescent vest, a completely absurd idea; eventually we would take the vest and cut the number out and pin it on our bags and complying with the law, we were still "showing our numbers." But this asshole was pulling all of this out in front of the cop. I hadn't gotten my license, I hadn't gotten my number. The cop now became interested in me. Now I was at fault here, because of some law that had just been passed. The cop wanted to get all my information, and I wasn't about to give it to him.

I picked up my bike and started walking down Summer Street towards South Station. The cop was on duty and really couldn't leave, and the guy was now screaming every obscenity he could think of at me. I had to get on my radio, and I called in. "131, here, Tony do you copy?" "131, what the hell happened, are you alright? I've got jobs for you."

"Yeah, well, they'll have to go to someone else, I'm down, my day's over, I'll call you on the phone." " 10-4. " So I'm walking down the street and I see a friend of mine, Tommy, who's driving a delivery van. "Tommy," I start screaming at him and he sees me and the state of my bike, and he's like, "Do you need a ride?" I throw my bike in his van and say, "Drive, just go, I'll tell you all about it." Tommy really rescued me that day. I think the owner of the car was still ranting and raving when we drove off. Tommy took me on a couple of his drop offs and then back home (really to the bar near my home). I had to scrap a bike together for work and in a few days I was back on the job.

Once I was delivering a package to a realtor, and as it turned out, he was being sued for something big. I was bringing bad news and the guy freaked out on me, threatened me, and grabbed me by my bag and started pushing me around. I knocked his hands off me and was really pissed but couldn't do anything about it, so I stormed out of this office and called my dispatch, who told me to go back up there and deliver it again. I called my office on the phone and explained the whole thing. They in turn called the law office sending the package and had me come back to their office, where I gave them consent and they recorded the whole story as I told it to them, thanked me, and told me they were sorry for the whole thing, but that my story would most likely help them win the case. I left with no tip.

There is a real fraternity among messengers, but that kinship is earned, and when you're a rookie, you're just that: A Rookie. The older messengers don't give you the time of day, and it's not that that's wrong, because I did just the same thing to Rookies as I became seasoned. And it's not like you're doing anything deliberate to hurt or misguide anyone, you just don't need to think about anything other than making your money. And if you're working for a company and not yourself, it's not a lot of money, so you have to bust your ass to get as many jobs as you possibly can. It's fiercely competitive, and I remember that there was this one company that paid their messengers better, and all their jobs were downtown to downtown (i.e. very easy) and I hated those kids, and not only that, but they were assholes. They thought they were better than everybody else because they were making more money, and they had it real cushy, so there was this animosity there. But as I became more of a veteran, I had my circle of friends and we'd do things like "two fingers," a basic handshake where you put out two fingers as you ride past someone you know and they slap them

> We all did the same shit for work and we would tell horror stories...

with two fingers as well. There was a lot of that type of stuff going on, and when Friday would come we'd all go into the bar and drink and let loose, and it was a really cool time. We all did the same shit for work and we would tell horror stories, like that one about the guy being subpoenaed not signing for the package and insulting me. As we were in the bar drinking, I'm thinking I'm going to throw a brick through his office window because he was such an asshole to me, but you know, of course, I didn't do it. But that's kind of the way it was.

The last straw had to be the weather. And the fact that the money wasn't so good. I'd go home wet and freezing so many times and go and deposit my check thinking "fuck this." I was in a band for a while doing this job and dreaming dreams of grandeur as a rock star and all that, and I wrote a song. Here is a sample:

Never Gonna Learn

Get on the Bike and Ride through the day

Gotta drop it off gotta make it pay

And in the rain it'll get even worse

Snowing and sleeting sometimes it's a curse

And You're Going up the lift with the monkeys in suits

You know sometimes they all look like fools

You could be such a superstar

If you don't get hit by a car

And you're never gonna, never gonna, you're never gonna learn

People walking out from behind parked cars

Taxi drivers never try and look too hard

Now you see this bus coming straight for you

Tell me what the fuck do you plan to do

And you're up on the sidewalk to spread some fear

All the nervous people are trying to stand clear

Jump the curb and you're almost gone

Gotta get out before too long

And you're never gonna, never gonna, you're never gonna learn

Chris Seifert/StalkersMusic Inc.

No Secrets
Mr. Mahi with Leah Ryan

Q: How long have you worked at this restaurant?

A: For 13 years.

Q: And you started as a busboy?

A: Yes.

Q: And you're still a busboy?

A: Yes. Sometimes the boss says he wants to give me a promotion, but I ignore him.

Q: Really? Why?

A: I like to sleep in the morning. It is a good opportunity for me.

Q: Waiters have to come in early?

A: Yes, and also, when there is one or two tables, I can leave early.

Q: Do you have a family?

A: I am married and I have a boy and a girl, two and three.

Q: What do you like best about the job?

A: Going home early.

Q: Did you work at another restaurant before this one?

A: Yes, but not as good. Waiters were always saying, "Get water for the table!"

Q: You mean yelling at you?

A: Yes. The managers know that busboy is the worst job. Sometimes they would say, "Shut up, busboy!"

Q: But you've been here for 13 years. Why?

A: *(holds up hand)* Same human being. Same five fingers. Different mentality. The waiters here are always having good behavior. And the gay and lesbian people, I can't explain how nice.

Q: You mean the gay and lesbian people who work here?

A: Yes *(begins long list of names)*.

Q: What about customers? What are they like?

A: Sometimes regular customers leave good tips for me.

Q: Because they know you.

A: The customers here have good behavior. But last Friday a man was with his wife -- I took the drink order. A waiter was coming out of the door and I did this *(leans over)*. The man said, "I want the manager!" He thought I was trying to get in front of his wife. He sees what he sees, but he doesn't know my heart.

Q: Are there any secrets at this restaurant?

A: No. No secrets. I am open. I am telling everything.

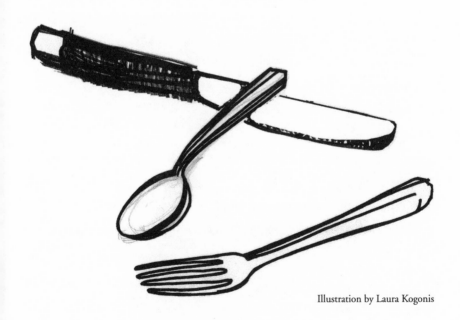

Illustration by Laura Kogonis

TURN OFF THE CELL PHONE, BARRICADE THE DOOR, BURN YOUR BILLS, SMASH YOUR TELEVISION, SET FIRE TO THE BIG BOX RETAILER THAT IS LOWERING WAGES FOR EVERYONE...

AND CATCH UP ON YOUR READING!

GC PRESS